Meet Me At The Well is for every woman who has ever tried to be all things to everyone and, more often than not, ends up spiritually dehydrated. Virelle Kidder is a master storyteller. Her transparent, captivating writing, coupled with God's enduring wisdom, offers a refreshing dive into God's word you cannot afford to miss.

> Carmen Leal, author of *The Twenty-Third Psalm for Caregivers* and founder of SomeOne Cares Christian Caregiver Conferences

Meet Me At The Well is not just another Christian book. It's a way of life. This book shows us how to be safe in God's arms . . . to really, really believe He is there at the well for us every day.

> Patricia Lorenz, inspirational writer and speaker; author of ten books, including *Life's Too Short To Fold Your Underwear* (Guideposts Books) and one of the top contributors to the *Chicken Soup for the Soul* books

Through *Meet Me at the Well,* Virelle Kidder lets us into her life and takes us with her on a month-long journey to dig down to our common source of Living Water. There we are directed to the Word and the truth that He is there, and will meet us, no matter what. I found her message real, warm, and reassuring, and I know many others will too.

> Nancie Carmichael, former editor of *Virtue Magazine* and author of *Selah: Your Moment to Stop, Think, and Step into Your Future*

Virelle Kidder's *Meet Me at the Well* is far from a thirst quencher. Rather, her stories of the draining everyday stresses we all face and the end of her spiritual drought show her readers that they too are welcome at the Living Well. Her gentle daily guides to replenishing the soul refresh . . . and fire the desire for deepening our relationship with Christ.

Melanie Rigney, editor

In her book *Meet Me at the Well: Take a Month & Water Your Soul,* Virelle Kidder openly addresses the struggles we face and voices the concerns we're hesitant to admit: I'm afraid . . . I'm angry . . . I'm tired. Her 30-day program, complete with real-life examples and biblical truth, helps us recognize the symptoms of spiritual, emotional, and physical drought and then points us to the only true source of healing—the Living Water, Jesus.

Vonda Skelton, speaker and author of *Seeing Through the Lies: Unmasking the Myths Women Believe*

If you've ever felt all dried up from the duty and demands of life, then dive into Virelle Kidder's *Meet Me At The Well*! These beautifully written devotions will splash healthy doses of serenity and sanctuary all over you—offering both refreshment and renewal. To soak up God's love and faithfulness in your soul, jump right in—the water's fine!

Lucinda Secrest McDowell, speaker and author of *Role of a Lifetime*

If life has ever left you feeling so completely dehydrated that you could be blown away by even the slightest breeze, then this book is for you. Virelle's book is an oasis in the desert. It provides a cool, refreshing drink for a parched soul. Drawing from the arid experiences in her life, Kidder takes the reader on an exciting journey of faith and will introduce the reader to the One who can satisfy every thirst.

Linda Moore, director, By Design Ministries

Meet Me at the Well: Take a Month & Water Your Soul is most appropriately named, as it truly is a refreshing yet gentle plunge into the Source of Living Water. Virelle aptly reminds us, through open and honest revelations of her own foibles and failures, how desperately we need to drink of the Savior's life. If you're stressed, tired, weary, worn-out, frustrated, on-the-edge-and-ready-to-fall off, call a time out and make a thirty-day commitment to meet the Life Giver at the well and to drink of the living water He so freely offers. You'll come away feeling renewed and refreshed—and glad you took the plunge.

Kathi Macias, author of twenty-one books, including *Beyond Me: Living a You-First Life in a Me-First World* (New Hope Publishers, 2008)

If you are busy, overwhelmed, or exhausted, meet Virelle Kidder at the well where she will splash the soothing, cooling water of life, joy, and refreshment on your dry soul. Enjoy Virelle's beautiful writing, great storytelling, and deep insights from one who has been where you are. Drink deeply.

Karen Porter, author of *I'll Bring the Chocolate, Satisfying a Woman's Cravings for Friendship and Faith.*

Pure joy! Encouraging us to live life to the fullest, Virelle welcomes us into her life. Offering her hand as a best friend, she leads us deep into the well to take a fresh drink from the Man whose fountain will never run dry. You'll fall in love with life, Virelle, and the Man at the well.

Elaine W. Miller, speaker and author of *Splashes of Serenity: Bathtime Reflections for Drained Moms* and *Splashes of Serenity: Bathtime Reflections for Drained Wives*

Refreshing as only a cool drink on a hot summer day can be, *Meet Me at the Well* by Virelle Kidder refreshes the soul. After gulping the book down whole, I look forward to going back and sipping it a day at a time. On every page Kidder shows us that God is, that He loves us, that He wants us to love Him, and that He wants to be our Living Water. May we all "Meet at the Well." We will find our souls well-watered! A must for everyone who has ever gone through a desert or even felt parched in their relationship with the Lord.

Deb Haggerty, author and speaker

With warmth and honesty, Virelle Kidder invites us to the spiritual well—not only to drink deeply of hope and love but to rest in our heavenly Father's lap. Read *Meet Me at the Well* and be refreshed.

Sandra P. Aldrich, author and speaker

MEET ME AT THE WELL

TAKE A MONTH & WATER YOUR SOUL

VIRELLE KIDDER

MOODY PUBLISHERS
CHICAGO

All scripture quotations, unless otherwise indicated , are taken from the *Holy Bible, New International Version*®. NIV®. Copyright ©1973, 1978, 1984 by International Bible Society. Used by permission of Zondervan. All rights reserved.

Scripture quotations marked TNIV are taken from the *Holy Bible, Today's New International Version* TNIV®. Copyright© 2001, 2005 by International Bible Society. Used by permission of Zondervan. All rights reserved.

Scripture quotations marked KJV are taken from the King James Version.

Editor: Cheryl Dunlop
Interior Design: Ragont Design
Cover Design: The DesignWorks Group, Jason Gabbert
Cover Image: Photos.com #22477988

Library of Congress Cataloging-in-Publication Data

Kidder, Virelle.
    Meet me at the well : take a month and water your soul / Virelle Kidder.
      p. cm.
    ISBN-13: 978-0-8024-4861-3
    ISBN-10: 0-8024-4861-5
    1. Christian women--Religious life. I. Title.

  BV4527.K474 2007
  242'.643--dc22

                              2007028389

We hope you enjoy this book from Moody Publishers. Our goal is to provide high-quality, thought-provoking books and products that connect truth to your real needs and challenges. For more information on other books and products written and produced from a biblical perspective, go to www.moodypublishers.com or write to:

Moody Publishers
820 N. LaSalle Boulevard
Chicago, IL 60610

1 3 5 7 9 10 8 6 4 2

Printed in the United States of America

To Steve, whose love is so like God's

CONTENTS

FOREWORD

For years I carefully balanced being a wife, a mom, a church leader, a writer, and a speaker. I subconsciously equated a full calendar with a successful personal and spiritual life. I made goal charts of what I wanted to accomplish over a five and ten year period. I dreamed big dreams and enjoyed brainstorming with creative people who were passionate about pursuing worthwhile projects.

Then a single phone call tipped the scales of my focused life, and my carefully planned future turned upside down. Our son, a U.S. Naval Academy graduate with an impeccable record and a promising future, was arrested for the murder of his wife's first husband.

The biological father of our son's stepdaughters, a man with multiple allegations of abuse against him, appeared on the brink of getting unsupervised visits with two vulnerable little girls. Our son unraveled emotionally, mentally, and spiritually, and after two and a half years and seven postponements of his trial, he was eventually convicted of murder and sentenced to life without the possibility of parole. (You can read the complete story in *A New Kind of Normal.*)

I entered the driest spiritual season of my life. My eyes were wet with tears, but my soul was in a drought. I couldn't find my way to the well of Living Water. Scripture verses I had cherished seem buried in the distant memories of a much happier past. A cloud of depression settled over my head, and in my spirit I felt far away from the once intimate relationship I had with God. I tried to read the Bible and found myself having to read the same verses over again because I was too emotionally exhausted to comprehend what I was reading. Simple tasks drained me of energy.

Prayer had always been a delight—a running conversation between God and me. Now praying was an effort, with me wondering if my desperate pleas actually made it to their intended destination. People e-mailed me Scripture, but my head could not comprehend any more verses about how much God loves me or about how His compassions are new every day. I was in a desert place—and when you are in that dry, thirsty place, sometimes it feels easier to quit trying to get closer to God because you are too tired emotionally and spiritually to make the effort.

No doubt you do not have a son who has been sentenced

to spend the rest of his life in prison, but pain is pain is pain is pain. It's all pain. And when the life you anticipated turns out to be far different from the life you are living, you no longer feel strong enough, nor do you have the desire to investigate how to water your soul and experience the spiritual refreshment you once knew. You may be caught between caring for aging parents and meeting the demands and needs of your adult children. You may be the mother of young children and the demands of your job have robbed you of any extra time for a meaningful devotional experience. You could be the only responsible sibling in your family and everyone looks to you to make decisions, avert disasters, and handle "irregular" relatives.

You're worn out, tired of the unfairness of caring for so many people, and God seems far away. You're a bit like the woman on the front of a greeting card who says: "When life begins to overwhelm me, I take a relaxing drive in the country. I'm now 2,600 miles away from home." The trouble is, you have no real destination if you run away, but you're dying on the vine, longing for the joy you once experienced as a Christian woman who embraced God's love.

The good news is in this book. Virelle Kidder understands how you feel and she admits she's even been angry about what God has allowed to happen in her life. Her authenticity gives credibility throughout this remarkable month-long journey to spiritual refreshment. The beauty of *Meet Me at the Well* is that it is designed so you can read one short chapter a day, and no matter how busy you are, you can accomplish that. At the end of each daily reading, there is a Scripture passage fully written out, followed by a section called Today's Replenishment.

There you will find practical ways you can apply what you just read.

If you're thirsty for a relationship with God that is healthy and growing, commit to reading this book—one chapter a day —for the next month. Write out the verses at the end of each chapter on a sticky note and place that note where you can read it several times that day. Then take a few minutes to take the suggested action step in the replenishment section at the end of the chapter. The delightful result, should you choose to take this assignment, will be a renewed relationship with the One who loves you best. *Meet Me at the Well* will refresh your soul and satisfy your thirst for Him. I highly recommend this book!

Carol Kent, speaker and author of
A New Kind of Normal

ACKNOWLEDGMENTS

I figure that God and my dear husband, Steve, will read these notes of enormous gratitude written on my heart, so I will thank them first. No one but my heavenly Father could have carried me through these years, set me upright again, and renewed me down to my toes with a fresh yearning to sing His love song to the world. I pray I never stop singing it. Thank You, Father, for renewing my heart and allowing me to write this devotional book. I pray You will bring it to the hands of those who need it. Thank You, especially, for sparing Steve's life this past year and allowing me more time with him.

Steve, whom everyone knows is the best man on the face of the earth, is God's daily gift to me. His gentleness, humor, strength, kindness, and love for more than forty years have made me a rich woman. I pray our sons and grandsons will all be like their dad and papa. I'm happy to be his girlfriend for the rest of my life. He's also combed through this book checking for errors, shed tears along the way, and chuckled encouragement. Thank you, Steve, for endless hours of listening, praying, encouraging, making me laugh, editing, and learning to cook once in a while. I hardly dare tell other writers how easy I have it. We're a team!

To my agent, Steve Laube, go multiplied thanks for being an outstanding professional and a prayerful, godly man. You've sharpened my focus more than you know.

After I delivered this message as a ten-minute devotional for AWSA sisters in Denver, Peg Short said, "I need this book. When can you write it?" Thank you, Peg.

To Carol Kent, thank you for your riveting words, "I want you to put this into a four-session retreat." And I shall. Thank you for graciously writing the foreword to this book.

A big thank-you goes to my adult-kids-turned-best-friends, to all the patient people in my life who prayed and seldom saw me, and to Dave and José who provided me with a friendly new MacBook and printer.

To the Moody Publishers team: Jennifer Lyell, Rhonda Elfstrand, both editorial and marketing pros, plus Moody's artists, designers, publicists, and many more, go my thanks for shepherding this message into a living thing. Thank you, Cheryl Dunlop, for such thoughtful editing. May it sing of His love!

Last but hardly least, grateful thanks to my on-line writing buddies: Michele Huey, Christa Parrish, and Melanie Rigney. Your honest critiques and prayerful words of encouragement kept me on target and set me free. May God fling your writing beyond your dreams.

I'M DYING HERE, LORD

I'm no Wonder Saint. You're not either? Good.

If you find yourself currently overwhelmed by your responsibilities, torn in two by the needs of others, or waking up begging for strength to get you through the next day, then we might be related. Do people count on you to be strong but your emotional tank was empty long ago? I bet you wonder why God gave you more than you could possibly accomplish in one day, maybe a lifetime? Ever want to quit?

I'm your queen. May I be honest?

I'm done in. Over the past eight or ten years, waves of heavy responsibility pounded my life. An exploding ministry workload already filled the calendar when suddenly

family members with serious chronic illness and disastrous problems began sucking up every moment of my time. Add to the mix my husband's outside ministry load, planning several weddings, plus a few irritating health issues of my own, and you've got a midlife woman wanting to run away in the middle of the night. You too?

I thought that was not supposed to happen to strong Christians. If we're in the Word every day and all "prayed up," aren't we supposed to suck it up and go on forever? Yes, we often do. Right to an early grave.

I heard a friend say once, "Beauty may be skin-deep, but stupid runs clear through!" But stupid can seem so right, so "spiritual," can't it? I only half listened to friends who cautioned me about overload, overwork, too much stress and responsibility. That's another name for pride.

If you're just the teensiest bit uncomfortable, stop a minute and look at yourself honestly in the mirror. Forget the wrinkles; look behind your eyes. Is the woman you see anxious? Are her lips pursed? Has she neglected her appearance? What do others see? Someone who's worn around the edges, fragile emotionally, sluggish mentally, just a tad nervous and critical of herself and others? I fit all of the above not that long ago.

People we really love, plus our responsibilities, can suck the life out of us when we're not looking. They can sap our joy, that energetic love for God that once leaped inside us just thinking about Him. Without it, life simply weighs more and discouragement and depression slither in uninvited. In no time, we feel like a hopeless mess.

Two summers ago I walked into my doctor's office with hives. Actually, I had chest pains too, and a jaw that was acting up. I was tired and feeling old. Just before I left the house, my wise husband, Steve, had said, "Tell Dr. Mastroianni I think you're depressed." I told the doctor, adding a weak chuckle.

"I knew it the minute you walked in the door." His gray mustache curled around a smile. "And it's about time!" he added.

"What on earth do you mean?" I asked as he pumped up the blood pressure cuff.

"Look at your life, Virelle," he said, and then listened quietly to the stethoscope for a moment. "Blood pressure's a little high too. Look at what you've been through the last few years. Did you think you were immune?" I guess I did.

This much-loved doctor knew our family well. It's true, we'd had a lot of "stuff" to deal with. I suppose it began many years earlier with a prodigal son (who's wonderful now, praise God!), then a child who struggled with regular bouts of mental illness, another daughter with lupus, a son with a heart problem, my own repeated surgeries, Steve's stressful job, financial challenges during and following the college years and five weddings, both our efforts at ministry, and now my mother's recent diagnosis with Alzheimer's and all that has accompanied it. I'd become so used to living with toxic levels of stress, I thought it was normal. You too?

"What do you do to relax?" my doctor probed gently. "Anything fun?"

"Well, I love to read." Come to think of it, I read only serious nonfiction books.

"Do you exercise?"

"Not enough really." I used to walk and swim laps, but no time anymore, I'm ashamed to admit. "But I pray a lot!"

"That's good, but it's not helping much, is it?" He didn't mean to hit below the belt, but he was right. Why wasn't my prayer life helping much? Was my faith weak? Sitting in his office, now I felt like a failure as a Christian too.

How stupid. How many times have I counseled others to take care of themselves physically, mentally, spiritually? How often have I reassured women to let God use any means He chooses to lovingly care for them and make them whole again? That's good advice for all but me, apparently.

"Too much stress, Virelle. You need to take care of yourself for a change." Dr. Mastroianni handed me a prescription for an antidepressant "just to take the edge off," he said gently. "See me again in a month or so. And get some rest." He smiled reassuringly. I dragged myself back home to tell Steve he was right.

It's not like God hadn't prepared me ahead of time for this. Many years ago on the second day of a retreat I was giving in Vermont, the conference director showed up at my door just before breakfast.

"In my devotions this morning, God told me to give this to you," she said, handing me a scrap of paper bearing a scribbled verse.

"Terrific! Let's see what it is." I read it out loud with interest. "As they make music they will sing, 'All my fountains are in you.' Psalm 87:7 Hmm."

"Does it mean anything to you?"

"Well, nothing's jumping out at me right now, but it's a

very nice verse. I'll pray about it." And I did. For years. Watch out when you do that.

Today its message is the central focus of my life. It should have been a long time ago.

Wait! I hear someone clucking, *Weren't you having your quiet time every day? You can't dry up when you're in the Word daily!*

I used to think that too, but now I see that body, mind, and spirit are one complete package. When one part suffers, the whole person suffers.

While on earth, Jesus met alone with His Father daily to drink deeply of the Water of Life. He taught His funny band of twelve the rhythm of coming away to rest and leave the madness behind.

In the last few years, I've written a lot about hearing God's voice at the unexpected corners of our journey. I usually expect His voice to be "still and small." I didn't know God ever shouted. How had I missed it? In a fresh read through the book of the Revelation, I stopped short at chapter 21: "And I heard a loud voice from the throne saying, 'Now the dwelling of God is with men, and he will live with them. They will be his people, and God himself will be with them and be their God. He will wipe every tear from their eyes. There will be no more death or mourning or crying or pain, for the old order of things has passed away'" (vv. 3–4).

When our heavenly Father lifts His voice magnificently down the centuries, it's best to listen well. He says, "'Come!' And let him who hears say, 'Come!' Whoever is thirsty, let him come; and whoever wishes, let him take the free gift of the water of life" (Revelation 22:17).

I was beyond thirsty, friends. I was parched. Lifeless, dry as a bone.

But not anymore. I found the well. Come on. I'll take you there.

LIVING WATER

"Come to me, all you who are weary and burdened, and I will give you rest. Take my yoke upon you and learn from me, for I am gentle and humble in heart, and you will find rest for your souls. For my yoke is easy and my burden is light."

MATTHEW 11:28–30

Today's Replenishment

Are you feeling drained like I was? If you're not, just wait awhile. People's needs wear us out as they did Jesus. Take a moment and list in your personal prayer journal all the things that drain you. (If you don't have a journal, get a notebook to keep with your Bible.) Be honest.

Tell God what you are thirsty for. Is it rest? Comfort? Order in your chaotic world, wisdom to make tough decisions, grace to let go, acceptance of unwanted change in your life? Don't try to dress things up in church clothes. Pour out your complaint to God and cry or rail on His shoulder. He loves you and He will listen.

Now commit yourself to coming daily to the well with me for the next month. I'll share my journey with you and you can share yours with God alone, or with a small group of believers if you choose. At the end of the month, I'd love to hear from you. You can write to me at connect@virellekidder.com. Let me know what God has done in your life. God will sing with joy over you as He promises in Zephaniah 3:17: "The LORD your God is with you, he is mighty to save. He will take great delight in you, he will quiet you with his love, he will rejoice over you with singing."

DO YOU SEE ME, JESUS?

Thirst is a good thing. It keeps us alive. Ask any mom with a newborn.

Our newest grandchild, Jack, was born one year ago in November. What a joy to hold a new baby! Tiny fingers and toes, gossamer eyelashes, delicate nose and mouth, soft downy hair. An amazing miracle. New babies are not shy when they're thirsty. Oh no, they let the whole world know! My daughter-in-law, José, laughs because every time Jack hears her voice, he opens his mouth.

How quickly we forget to come to the Source of Life, open our spirits wide, and drink deeply. We need reminding. I know I did.

Move back in time with me and get reacquainted with a woman so contemporary it's uncanny. We know her as the woman at the well in John 4. I call her Moriah. Here's the VSV (Virelle's Standard Version) of her story.

Moriah was well acquainted with thirst. The trouble was, she'd drunk at every shallow stream. A string of husbands couldn't make her happy; in fact, she'd tell you the worthless bums made her more miserable. Her money was gone. Respect was out the door; "good women" didn't do what she'd done. She'd have been a perfect fit in twenty-first-century America! But alas, Moriah lived in Samaria, not a forgiving place . . . until one day when she went out to get water at Jacob's well at high noon, when all the good women were at home. Moriah showed up with her pitcher, and Jesus sat waiting for her. He was thirsty too, physically thirsty.

Meeting Jesus is seldom convenient. He doesn't make an appointment. He just shows up and often asks us to do something radical, like change our whole life.

When she saw Him, Moriah must have wanted to turn around and come back later. But there He sat. There was nothing to do but go forward and deal with the situation. Moriah strode up to the well and lowered her bucket until she heard a splash. And then He spoke.

"May I have something to drink?" He asked.

She stared at him a moment. "I thought you couldn't ask Samaritans like me for a drink."

"If you knew how generous God is, you'd have asked Me for a drink and I'd have given you living water."

Is He trying to make a fool out of me? "Say, You haven't even got Your own bucket, and You think You're going to get living water out of this well? Don't You know Jacob gave us this well? Are You better than him?"

In the broad sunlight Jesus looked different from the other men she'd known, like He wasn't trying to get something from her. He responded calmly, "You can keep drinking this water as long as you want, and you'll still be thirsty, but anyone who drinks the water I offer will never thirst again—not ever. In fact, she'll have a new well inside herself that bubbles over with eternal life."

A very strange man, this one. "Give me some of this water so I won't have to keep coming back here every day."

"Go get your husband," He replied. "I'll wait right here."

She turned to face him squarely "I haven't got one."

"That's exactly right. In fact, you've had five of them, haven't you? And the man you're with right now—he's just a boyfriend, isn't he?" Moriah nearly stopped breathing for a second. Then she came at Him with all four barrels.

"So You're a prophet, huh? Well, tell me this, if our forefathers worshiped God right here, why do you Jews say worship should take place only in Jerusalem? Answer me that!"

What He next said confused her, something like, "The kind of people God wants to worship Him will worship Him in spirit and truth." Her mind began to blur. She felt vulnerable, afraid of this man. He knew her. But how?

Haltingly she responded, "I know the Messiah is coming. He'll explain all these mysteries to us."

Jesus spoke again quietly. "Look no further. I am He."

Tears stung her eyes as Moriah dropped her bucket and

ran back to her home, ran to tell the townspeople about Him, ran to find herself for the very first time. And when she told them, they came to see for themselves. Best of all, they believed her.

In my mind, Moriah is a rock star. She's a sinful woman, and she knows it. Facing ourselves honestly, sins and stupidity included, is huge. It's also the launchpad for renewal.

Moriah didn't lie, hide behind her problems, or play the victim. No more games with this woman. Moriah was no hypocrite. I like that.

You and I need the same bold courage. No masks, no pretending we're in better shape than we are. Just tell Him the truth: We're bone-dry.

After being a Christian more than thirty years, the truth was I *wasn't* able to handle everything on my plate, but I was making myself sick trying. I thought God would take me through, but this time was different. I just wanted to cry and run away from life. I'd thought I was a maturing Christian, but now I wasn't so sure. How could I be and feel this way?

Did you know it's entirely possible to be desperately thirsty in body, mind, and spirit and not know it? I've hardly met a woman who hasn't been there at least once.

Jesus experienced deep thirst too. He was thirsty to do the will of God, something otherworldly. Thirsty to bring His Father praise and honor and worship, to bring songs of joy to the throne of God. Not even His disciples knew what that meant until later.

We aren't born with that kind of thirst. We're reborn with it. The greatest joy in our journey toward renewal is recovering our thirst for God's glory, our own song of praise to Him.

You may not feel ready to sing anything today. No one does when she is flat-out. Add a dose of depression to the mix, and you have one songless canary. For now, know that your song is coming. It is unique to you, a special gift from God.

Like Moriah, our coming to the well together is no accident. God arranged this meeting. Here's fair warning: Meeting Jesus can be pretty inconvenient. He stops your life and offers you a choice: Go back to your old routine, your own dead existence, or come to Him and find real Life.

Just as Jesus knew Moriah personally, He knows each one of us. He knows our names, our histories, our secret sins, our dreams, our pain. Nothing is hidden from Him. Do you know Him? If you are not certain, put this book down and take a step you'll never regret. You can invite Jesus to come into your heart right now, to forgive all your sins and be your Lord and Savior. And He will. Just like that. You can pray simply, "Lord Jesus, I've turned away from You a long time, but I want to come back. I ask You to forgive my sins. Thank You for dying for me on the cross. Come into my heart, Lord, and make me Your child. Show me how to live for You from this day onward without looking back. Amen."

If this was your prayer, welcome home, child. All of heaven is rejoicing over you right now! Your renewal has just begun.

For those who may have known the Lord for a very long time like me, but need renewal, you can begin the process with a simple prayer. "Lord, I'm thirsty and tired. I need You like never before. Lead me to a quiet place of rest with You now and teach me to listen to You with a quiet heart."

Praise God! Your renewal has just begun!

LIVING WATER

"Therefore, if anyone is in Christ,
he is a new creation;
the old has gone, the new has come!"

2 CORINTHIANS 5:17

Today's Replenishment

What small streams have you been drinking from
lately? Streams that don't satisfy can be things like
food, the stock market, shopping, success, love
relationships, a competitive spirit, even ministry in
overdrive. None of these is bad, but they don't
satisfy or help us become like Christ.
They aren't living water.

When I get dry, I've usually been supplementing
my spiritual thirst at a few of these streams before I
realize my spirit is about to drop. But God's
amazing grace meets me on my journey and says,
"Child, you're looking in all the wrong places.
Come to Me and drink."

Psalm 63:1 echoes our cry: "O God, you are my
God, earnestly I seek you; my soul thirsts for you,
my body longs for you, in a dry and weary land
where there is no water." Verses like this help me
realize that God isn't a bit surprised when I feel
overwhelmed and dry. It comforts me that He's not
supremely disappointed when I cave in.
Just like newborn Jack, I'm born to be thirsty,
to need His living water daily so
I can be a well bubbling up for others.

Before our time tomorrow, write out a prayer to
your loving Father in heaven. Confess all the ways
you've been looking elsewhere in smaller streams.
Ask Him to renew you one day at a time.

I'm So Tired of People Needing Me

I never imagined that white linoleum floors and folding tables and chairs could feel warm, even welcoming, but sitting in the nursing home activity room listening to a soft-spoken geriatric specialist explain my mother's diagnosis washed unbelievable comfort over me. Her compassionate understanding of my mother's disintegrating life surprised me, especially her knowledge of the ways it tangled and trapped mine into a hopeless knot.

At least eight or ten years had passed not knowing my mother had Alzheimer's. By then, she was already in Stage Two, mostly incontinent, refusing help, calling me ten or fifteen times a day. She presented a sweet exterior to a lucky few, but fired angry accusations and demands at me daily. In her mind, I had become the enemy.

It felt oddly familiar. Mental illness dotted our family tree for two generations or more. Early on I'd learned to read the emotions in a room before entering. *What just happened here? Dare I say what's on my mind?* My father's untreated bipolar illness dominated our home life, and now it tormented our daughter Amy decades later. Some days were wonderful, others like layovers in hell. After she returned to our home from a five-year abusive marriage, Steve and I once again absorbed her agony and emotional pain. We lifted and encouraged her through each day, praying for relief and healing. Eventually, it came as Amy's deep faith and courageous acceptance leveled out the deep valleys of her illness. I often walked a daily tightrope strung between two desperately hurting women I loved, my mother and my daughter.

Perhaps I didn't recognize the slow advance of Alzheimer's because I didn't want to believe it, or because distorted thinking can appear almost normal at first. Finally, Mother was hospitalized for a minor issue, and doctors recommended a thorough mental health exam at a nearby Alzheimer's research and care facility. Although only an autopsy proves the illness conclusively, her diagnosis was easily confirmed by a host of other symptoms. We were on a downhill slope that was headed nowhere good. The social worker equipped us well to adjust Mother's home and lifestyle to her increasing care needs, but I was unable to enforce change. I hired caregivers and within a week or two Mother fired them. I was stuck.

With the best intentions, women often take on, or are left with, others with huge needs. Why? Because we feel it's our job. And no one else has volunteered. Whether we ought to do the caregiving or not, our response is powerful and emotional. But caring for others' deep needs exhausts us to our core. There's a limit to how much anyone can do.

Want relief?

There's no sin in it. Jesus knew the feeling well.

People wore Jesus out regularly, especially the twelve who walked, ministered, fished, and ate every meal with Him. Why was their understanding and faith so small after all this time? He was incredulous. One such incident is recorded in Mark 9.

Jesus climbed one of the highest mountains in Galilee to be alone with Peter, James, and John. I rode up this mountain a few years ago in stark terror as our van driver careened around unguarded hairpin turns, gunning the engine harder with each curve. I wondered if he was driving us straight to heaven. Jesus knew where to get His disciples alone with Him. No one but a wild goat would have followed them up there.

Calling it a life-changing event doesn't even cover what happened. When Jesus allowed these three to see Him in all His glory talking with Elijah and Moses, Peter wanted to turn the spot into a religious tourist attraction. God had a better idea, spoken from the brilliant cloud to their quaking hearts, "This is my Son, whom I love. Listen to him!" (verse 7). And they did.

Scarcely had the glow of the moment faded when they arrived back down the mountain. Here a crowd clustered around the waiting nine disciples, now in a heated argument with local religious teachers over why they could not cast a demonic presence out of a very needy boy.

For Jesus, that was the last straw.

"O unbelieving generation," Jesus replied, "how long shall I stay with you? How long shall I put up with you? Bring the boy to me" (Mark 9:19). I picture a hush coming over the crowd; nine disciples staring down at the sand. They'd tried everything they knew and had failed again.

It is the father's honest confession that helps me. "If you can do anything, take pity on us and help us!"

"'If you can'?" Jesus cast a riveting look at the heartbroken father. "Everything is possible for him who believes."

With that the father fell to his knees and cried out, "I do believe; help me overcome my unbelief!"

Help me overcome mine, Lord, when I can't see past the problem. I'm blinded by fear that if You don't change things, I'll be in this circumstance for the rest of my life!

Is that your prayer right now? What if God leaves you as you are and doesn't change things? Jesus read the mind of the stricken father as He does ours. We know what happened next. He rebuked the evil spirit who, shrieking, left the boy limp and near death. Then Jesus reached down and lifted him by the hand to a new life, a real life for the first time.

Ever wonder why Jesus wrestled so with the disciples' pretty marginal unbelief? After all, they tried hard, and they were seriously committed to Him. They'd left all to follow Him. Wasn't that belief enough? What more did He want?

I think He wanted the same honest confession that came from the boy's father. When my faith falters, it's no surprise to God. Confession releases my fear and brokenness and brings welcome relief and hope. It puts the outcome totally out of my hands and into His merciful ones. Blessed relief!

Need relief from the crushing needs you face daily? Do the people God has given you to care for wear you out too? Bring them to Him again. Confess your fears and shaky faith. See what God will do.

LIVING WATER

"Come with me by yourselves to a quiet place and get some rest."

MARK 6:31

Today's Replenishment

Do you identify more with the father in the story
or his son? Each of them found his life wrecked by
something over which he had no control, and
certainly did not deserve or bring on himself.

Perhaps people have prayed for you and nothing
changes. Why has God let you suffer so long? Do
you wonder if you've failed to pray right? We don't
always know. Just for today, try thanking God for
His power and love at work in your life even if you
don't see it now. Thank Him that He knows the
needs of those you love. They are His concerns
even more than yours. Do you believe that?

Read Psalm 139. God is before, behind, and way
ahead of every breath we take. What could possibly
please God more than being trusted with
everything that has you (and me) in knots today?
Write out a prayer and tell Him of your small faith.
Ask for the faith you need to face another day.

4

I Feel Angry at the Things You've Allowed

Shortly after September 11, 2001, I returned home from doing my radio talk show to find my husband, Steve, sitting on the couch waiting for me. "Better sit down," he said, patting the cushion next to him.

"What's wrong? What happened?" It had to be bad news. Steve never came home in the middle of the day.

"Something very bad," he said, his voice slow and faltering. He told me our oldest daughter, Lauren, had called him at work crying regarding her childhood friend Birgitta. "Birgitta died today giving birth to her fourth baby, a little girl."

"Not Birgitta! It can't be!" I clapped my

hand over my mouth and almost stopped breathing. "Not beautiful little Birgitta!" Tears followed in waves.

Lauren and her best friend had bounced around our house regularly, pretending to be twins. They loved giggling on the stairs in matching robes and pajamas, rolling their long blonde hair in big sock rollers. We all loved Birgitta, an only child of Swedish parents, and became the big family she didn't have. Her death was impossible to believe.

"Nobody dies in childbirth anymore. What could have happened?"

"She died of a blood clot. They couldn't save her."

Questions raced through my mind. "What about the baby?"

"It looks like she'll be okay. Her name is Catrina."

"Oh, Steve! This just can't be!" We held each other and sobbed.

Memories flooded back. We missed Birgitta and her parents so much when they moved away to the Boston area when the girls were eleven or twelve. A couple of summers Birgitta and Lauren spent time as counselor interns at Camp Cherith, a Christian girls' camp in the Adirondack Mountains. Then one year after she returned home, Birgitta was diagnosed with a potentially fatal autoimmune disease. Over her yearlong recovery, Lauren led a youth group prayer effort for her and Birgitta was finally healed. After all that, why would God allow her life to be suddenly cut short at only thirty-four? It seemed a cruel nightmare.

Lauren later told me tearfully on the phone, "Mom, last night Birgitta and I talked on the phone for forty-five minutes, laughing over our kids and sharing prayer requests, just like old times. She was in the hospital on bed rest for a few days but was planning to go home today. She sounded great. Then, sometime after midnight, something went gravely wrong and she died suddenly. They took the baby by Caesarean," she choked between sobs. "It doesn't seem real that she's already in heaven."

It wasn't at all fair. Birgitta had a husband and four little girls who all needed her. How would they live without such a loving mom? How would her parents, Sonny and Irene, survive without her? And Lauren? We all cried together, but inside my heart raged, *God, how could you allow this?*

Let's be honest—God can seem cruel in what He allows. What do committed Christians do when they are angry with God? Just let it go? Chalk it up to unsolved mysteries or the dark side of an otherwise loving God? I don't think so.

Many years ago I asked a wise older woman who had suffered much how she reconciled this issue. Her answer surprised me. "Go ahead and let your anger out at God when you feel it. What better place?" she assured me. "God loves you and He is big enough to take it." *Did I dare? Was that allowed?* The prospect frankly scared me. It felt sacrilegious.

Dragging myself to such honesty, though, was worse than having ten root canals. In our home growing up, anger was a dangerous emotion, especially my father's anger. It wasn't worth the risk of tipping the scales. My mother, brother, and I learned to keep a tight lid on our emotions. Being the youngest, my lid tended to be looser than everyone else's. But tell God I was angry? It sounded risky. Who was I to question the sovereignty of God? Job did, and God wasn't too thrilled with him.

There was a long period when our family went through a season of suffering from small stuff to big. One of our most trying experiences was our younger daughter's unexpected attack of mental illness. Desperate for help the first time she languished in a psychiatric ward, I knelt in prayer one morning begging God to heal her. My husband and I had cried until our eyes were swollen. We'd prayed and fasted with no apparent answer. Halfway through my prayer for her healing, I realized how angry I was with God. Suddenly I began railing at Him for allowing such undeserved pain and for letting us down. "What do You expect from us? Is this the requirement for discipleship—the intense suffering of our children? Go ahead and hurt me, but not my kids!"

Finally quiet and limp, I rested my head on the bed wondering if I had crossed the line. Suddenly an alarming new thought hit. What if God still didn't answer? What would I do? Give up on Him? I had to make a choice.

Where else would I go? What else did I want in life but to follow Christ and know Him? The truth was, nothing. I wanted nothing more than that. I overheard myself pray, "Even if You give me nothing that I ask, nothing I want, I'll still believe. I won't quit." He had won.

I'm not alone. Jesus has tough choices for all His disciples at times. When Jesus was teaching at the synagogue in Capernaum, an enormous crowd followed Him there, including many who had been among the five thousand He had fed earlier. His words fascinated them. He gave them miraculous food, but they wanted more. They wanted a further sign from heaven as to who He really was. Jesus answered that He was actually the Bread of Life and those who believed in Him would have eternal life.

Grumbling spread through the crowd. Many doubted all the healings He had done, not to mention the other miracles. Bread of Life? Who'd He think He was, Yahweh Himself?

Then, in the next breath, Jesus claimed, "Whoever eats my flesh and drinks my blood has eternal life and I will raise him up at the last day." That did it. Large numbers of His followers turned away. This was too much, too drastic, too physical. Eat His flesh and drink His blood? This was the price for eternal life? No way. They were out of there.

Standing now in a quiet synagogue, Jesus turned to the Twelve and asked softly, "You do not want to leave too, do you?" (John 6:67).

Peter, good man Peter, answered, "To whom shall we go? You have the words of eternal life. We believe and know that you are the Holy One of God" (John 6:69).

We never know how much rests on our faithfulness, do we? Imagine if Peter and the disciples had wavered. It would have been easy to leave when the others did. But they stayed. They held on. I'm thankful for that.

Where will you and I go when we are disappointed and angry over what God allows? Will we quit? Give up? Or will we exist like so many, weak and bitter all our lives, living only a form of faith, having no joy or growth, no song to sing? I don't want that, do you?

If you have the courage, let your anger out in the only

appropriate place, God's lap. Stay there and sob your heart
out. Tell Him everything. Then do whatever He tells you, even
if it's to wait a little longer. Commit the outcome to Him and
trust Him to do what is best.

LIVING WATER

*"For my Father's will is that everyone who
looks to the Son and believes in him shall
have eternal life, and I will raise him up
at the last day."*

JOHN 6:40

Today's Replenishment

■

I hope your journal is becoming a private place for
recording your prayers and listening to God's
insights and answers. Today let's begin by being
honest with ourselves and frank with God.
Make a list in your journal of things you may
still feel angry about. No one else will see it.
Tell God the truth. He already knows.

Next, ask Him to reveal any thorn in your spirit
that may need pulling out. What still hurts you and
causes you to trust God less, or maybe even want to
turn away? Do you feel He has asked you to do
something that's too hard, too painful or extreme?
Tell Him. Confess your feelings. Be radically
honest with God. You'll never regret it

I'm praying you'll trust Him with the hurt. Will
you take your stand with Jesus no matter what?
Write out a prayer and tell Him so.

5

I'M OUT OF STRENGTH AND OUT OF ANSWERS

It's impossible to figure out what God is doing.

When Lauren was twelve, her dear friend Birgitta spent months in the hospital and rehab following a life-threatening attack from a rare autoimmune disease. Lauren prayed and fasted for months for Birgitta. One Saturday morning she came into the kitchen and said, "Mom, I asked God to give me Birgitta's illness and let her get well."

I wanted to say, "Lauren, God doesn't do that," but instead, I put my arms around her, sensing God didn't want me to respond with a qualifier about how He works. Within a year, Birgitta followed a hard path to recovery and gradually became well again. Within ten years, Lauren had lupus, an autoimmune disease and a cousin to Birgitta's illness.

Did God answer Lauren's prayer by giving her lupus? Only He knows.

Shortly after Birgitta died during the birth of her fourth baby, Lauren became pregnant. This baby was a surprise. A big surprise. Having babies when you have lupus is, at best, risky. Lauren already had two miracle babies after waiting ten years. Thane, now five-and-a-half, and Jillian, three-and-a-half, were easier and more independent now. We all knew a third pregnancy could be dangerous. It had been a rough year following a lupus flare-up the previous winter that almost landed her on chemo. She was still depressed over Birgitta's death. The fact that her doctor strongly recommended no more babies didn't help either. We were all worried. To be honest, I feared she might die in childbirth just like Birgitta. I think the whole family did.

Lauren wrestled with depression. One day while reflecting on the prophet Elijah under the broom tree, she remembered he, too, had come through a long period of testing. He was spent and depressed. He wanted no more challenges, no more marching orders from God. Can't you hear him moan, "Just leave me alone, God. Let me crawl in a hole and die!"

Take a look with me at 1 Kings 17. Again, here's the VSV, the Virelle's Standard Version of the story.

If there were Bible superheroes, Elijah would be one. During his time, Israel had a king named Ahab who was evil to the core. He was more evil than any king before, worshiping Baal rather than God and deceiving his people with the same lie. Beyond that, Ahab married Jezebel, who was every man's worst nightmare. It was to this winning couple that God sent the prophet Elijah bearing horrible news: God was sending drought, years of it, on the land of Israel. Ahab was not happy with the announcement, but Jezebel wanted Elijah dead. Elijah wanted to run away and die quietly somewhere.

God cared for Elijah by sending him to a safe place, the Kerith Ravine, east of the Jordan. There He had lined up a willing flock of ravens to bring him his daily allotment of natural food we can only assume was not roadkill. I like to think it was fresh whole grains, bits of meat, or fruit in season. The brook itself provided delicious spring water. Elijah's assignment? Just rest, eat, drink, and listen to God.

Have you ever noticed how God can sound just like your mother? What's the first thing she used to say when you came home from college or work? "Just rest, sweetheart. Put your feet up. Here, I made your favorite dinner. Maybe you need a nap. You look tired. Let me take care of your laundry, dear." My mother always made my favorite dinner, meatloaf and mashed potatoes. My kids loved chicken divan or stromboli, Italian meatballs and pasta. Anything with lots of fat and carbs.

Let's just assume the ravens brought Elijah's favorite comfort food.

When the brook finally dried up, God spoke to Elijah again and sent him to a hungry widow in Zarephath who also needed a miracle. "I have commanded a widow in that place to supply you with food," God said. Now this widow and her son were destitute, right down to their last little handful of flour and a tiny bit of oil. What a strange person God chose to feed Elijah! Talk about impossible jobs.

"Go home and make a little bread for me, then make something for yourself and your son," Elijah directed the widow. He'd learned something about God at the Brook Kerith. God does what He promises. If God says something is to be done, there's no lack of supplies. Food appears from nowhere, oil and wine keep flowing; ravens bring good things to eat, bread keeps popping from the oven. The water is sweet. Still, I'd like to hear what she said on the way home.

Right now, you and I need a place to rest and be fed.

Let God take care of all the Ahabs and Jezebels out there. Even Elijah couldn't fight battles all the time. We need to get away from those whose needs, criticisms, problems, and demands wear us out.

God will find the right brook for you. He has it all ready, including the food. When someone offers their home for a visit, their cottage at the lake, or even to take your kids overnight, say, "Yes. I'll take it. Thank you!" Why deny others the pleasure of obedience?

Rest isn't laziness. It's opening your mouth wide and waiting to be filled. It's eating your mother's meatloaf, coming to the table like the starving kid she loves to spoil. Rest is a certain step toward renewal. I hope the ravens bring me popcorn.

Lauren opened her Bible to the same passage we just examined and allowed God to feed her, soothe her fears, drain her anger, and trust Him with the future. As her baby moved inside her, joy trickled back into her spirit. We heard it in her voice.

At the baby's first sonogram, Lauren and Michael watched the screen as the doctor cautiously examined her a very long time. Turning to them when he finished, his comments landed heavily.

"It's a female. And she has a cyst on her brain. We have to watch and see how it develops. It could be serious." Not what any parent wants to hear.

Leaving the hospital a short while later, Lauren turned to Michael and said, "This baby girl needs to be named Kerith Brook." Michael wholeheartedly agreed. They both knew Camp Cherith had been a special memory with Birgitta, and now the Brook Kerith in the Bible symbolized a surprise place of refreshment from God in a dry time. The name was a perfect fit.

Just before Christmas on December 19, 2003, we all welcomed little Kerith Brooke McGarry into the world, a perfectly healthy baby girl. Mama and baby, Daddy and big brother and sister, yea, even Nana and Papa, aunts and uncles and cousins, all celebrated big time! Today she's a delightful three-year-old with blonde ponytails like her mama had, a loud laugh like Nana's, and her father's Irish eyes.

Yes. God's answers are good, indeed.

LIVING WATER

"O God, you are my God, earnestly I seek
you; my soul thirsts for you, my body longs
for you, in a dry and weary land where
there is no water."

PSALM 63:1

Today's Replenishment

■

Has God allowed drought in your life? It's hard to imagine dryness as a good thing, but it can be. The royal invitation still stands: "Come, all you who are thirsty, come to the waters; and you who have no money, come, buy and eat!" (Isaiah 55:1).

In your journal today, list all the ways you are thirsty. Now open your spirit wide and ask God to quench your thirst in a surprising way. He will.

Are you in need of a rest like Elijah, like all God's children from time to time? Do you have a Kerith Brook somewhere? Taking a rest is a wise and spiritual thing. Ask God to provide the brook, the Bread of Life, and the Water of Life. Don't forget to thank the ravens. They are His messengers on a mission to care for you.

Share your need for R & R with a group of prayerful friends. By doing this, you allow them the joy of praying it into being, possibly providing it. Try not to say, "I'm fine. I can make it. I just need a day to myself." When someone offers, take it. The real giver is God. He wants to bless you.

6

My Love Is Almost Gone

Years ago I began to pray, "Lord, make me a loving woman." The truth was, one day I recognized how self-centered I'd become. I began noticing it in little ways at home: feeling irritated at interruptions, wanting to be complimented more when I thought I looked good, sneaking the last spoonful of peanut butter. As harmless as these things seem, they pointed to a bigger problem: I was still a "me first" woman. The remedy wouldn't be easy—learning to love others more than I loved myself.

It seemed a simple prayer at first. I mentioned it to God silently when Steve and I had our devotions, fully expecting God to zap me into a soft-spoken, loving woman when no one was looking. Instead, He surrounded me with needy people who nearly sucked the life out of me.

Ten years ago, when our youngest daughter Amy moved home after a disastrous first marriage, she was in the midst of a mental health crisis. At the same time, my mother began a steady descent into Alzheimer's, turning her from a cheerful, independent woman with many friends into an angry, dependent person I hardly recognized. Her path was littered with blown microwaves, telephones and answering machines that mysteriously never worked, bills left unpaid, missing credit cards, and a sickening smell that permeated her home. I hired outside help; she fired them, wanting me to do it all.

Mother loved her home and staunchly refused to leave. Since it was only ten miles away, I trekked back and forth daily. At home our daughter needed a patient listener, a comforter, as she dealt with fresh emotional pain. Suddenly our peaceful life stopped and I became a full-time caregiver, as did Steve. We saw no other choice but to set aside our plans, dreams, and privacy, and turn our attention toward our daughter and my mother, in that order. Amazingly, two weeks prior to this tsunami, Steve and I had signed a contract to coauthor a book on Christian involvement in public schools. Now writing looked impossible. (God can do anything! See *Getting the Best Out of Public Schools* [Broadman & Holman, 1998].)

Our three other kids worried over the way our life had changed. We were no longer free to join them for family events. Especially sad was missing the birth of our granddaughter Jillian. Steve's Christlike patience was a daily model to me. He was careful not to let his sorrow show.

During those years, we both learned how costly sacrificial love really is.

For starters, my own love proved pathetically small. It was stilted, calculating, given in token dribbles. The "me first" woman couldn't cut it anymore. One day, in a tearful prayer of confession over what a failure I'd become, I simply gave up trying and asked God to give me His love right when I needed it. Mine was long gone. If He didn't answer, I had nowhere else to turn.

I soon learned that sacrificial love isn't fun. It's like standing still and getting beaten up. I wanted to defend myself. How did Jesus keep doing that? He loved us with supernatural power, especially when He got beaten up. Could ordinary people love like that?

We get glimpses of sacrificial love throughout the Bible. Abraham showed it when he gave his me-first nephew, Lot, the choicest land. Later he agreed to sacrifice his own son, Isaac, in obedience to God's command. The emotional dynamics of that scene still make me cry. Queen Esther took her life in her hands to beg for the lives of her own people, the Jews. Young Mary willingly received God's announcement through the angel that she would bear the Son of the living God, knowing it would mean public disgrace and the possible loss of her own marriage plans.

On and on, God poured out His supernatural love through His children. Don't think for a minute they did it on their own. In every instance, God gave what they needed as they looked to Him. You and I can too.

Nowhere is pure love more clearly seen than in Christ's

death on the cross. He showed a spiritually dead world what love really is when He died on our behalf. He let the whole world know how much God loves us by breaking His own heart and offering His only Son, Jesus, as a love sacrifice for our sins.

Has anybody ever loved you more?

Is there anyone you and I cannot love with the same Jesus living inside us?

God was so good to allow that long season in my life. He enabled my husband and me to give until we thought we couldn't give any more. Out of His endless well of love He replenished us as the need arose. Rather than the problems driving us apart from each other, our marriage flourished during this time. What a great gift! But there was another.

For nearly thirty years I prayed for my mother's salvation. Even though she grew up in a churchgoing home, her faith seemed nonexistent. Whenever I mentioned God's plan of salvation, she recoiled.

One day Amy, whose life was now restored, stopped at Gram's house for a visit. She found Mother crying uncontrollably over the Motor Vehicle Bureau taking her license away. She was furious with me and thought I had done it. (I wish I had.) Amy knelt by her chair and said, "Gram, you really need to ask Jesus into your heart and let Him help you with all this." Miraculously, my mother agreed.

"Just repeat after me, Gram," Amy prayed, holding the wrinkled hands in hers. "Dear Jesus, I want You to be my Savior. Please come into my life and forgive my sins. Help me with all my problems. Thank You for dying on the cross for me to make me Your loved child. Amen." My mother was eighty-six when she celebrated her first spiritual birthday and became a true child of God.

On many occasions, God has given Amy a ministry of sacrificial love that made an eternal difference. It always does. Although my mother never changed much outwardly, I thank God daily for Amy's willingness to recognize a brief window of openness before Alzheimer's clouded Mother's mind more fully.

Seasons change, thankfully. In time, God lifted the load of sorrow, replacing it with a new season of rest and renewal that led to this book. I can't wait to tell you the rest of the story!

LIVING WATER

"Be imitators of God, therefore, as dearly loved children and live a life of love, just as Christ loved us and gave himself up for us as a fragrant offering and sacrifice to God."

EPHESIANS 5:1–2

Today's Replenishment

■

"I tell you the truth," Jesus said. "Whoever hears my word and believes him who sent me has eternal life and will not be condemned; he has crossed over from death to life" (John 5:24). If you are not certain today that you are God's child, make sure. Invite Christ into your life and record the date in your Bible. Tell a Christian friend. You'll be glad you did.

What a relief it is to "come clean" with God. Whether you are a new Christian or one who needs a fresh supply of love, God wants you to find that today. Simple prayers are best. You may borrow mine and make it your own, if you like.

Lord, I have not enough love for this huge need. I confess my pride, my self-centeredness, and my reluctance to serve. Forgive me, Lord, and give me what I need in You. Teach me how You think about others; let me feel what You feel. Fill me now with everything I need to do Your will. Thank You ahead of time for answering this prayer. Amen.

7

BUT THEY'RE SO UNGRATEFUL!

Steve and I sat on white wicker chairs on the sweeping Victorian porch of Father Joseph Girzone's secluded mountain retreat in Altamont, New York, savoring a postcard-lovely September setting. Early fall leaves swirled on the extensive lawns bordered by dense woodlands. I wanted to live there.

Girzone, a former Catholic priest whose *Joshua* fiction series became a bestseller, is now in his seventies with a worldwide ministry of Christian renewal. A renegade priest unfettered by most religious convention, he is both refreshing and disarming. As we talked over coffee, I noticed the intensity of his bright eyes and the way the sun shone on his thick white hair. He seemed interested in our concerns.

Since we lived nearby, Steve had asked to meet with Father Girzone for help launching a pro-family organization in New York State. We talked about the difficulties building support across faith communities in the Northeast. He understood well and offered several suggestions.

Of all the things Father Girzone said that morning, one phrase stands out in my mind. Yes, it would be hard, he said, but no matter how we were treated, "Take no offense."

Steve asked him to repeat it.

"Take no offense at anything. That's what Jesus did. You must do the same." A tall order for anyone, one we never forgot. In the years since that morning, his advice has affected every area of our lives.

Being a servant of the Lord carries you places you never imagined. Many are thrilling, others challenging, and a few quite frightening. They all involve ministering to people. Therein lies the rub.

Somewhere along the way we learned what Jesus already knew. People are often ungrateful. Only a few say thank you; most forget what you've done until their next big need. That doesn't wear well over time and is disappointing at best. Apparently there's nothing wrong with feeling disappointed. Jesus did.

On one occasion told in Luke 17, Jesus was walking south toward Jerusalem from Galilee, passing along the border of Samaria when he heard men shouting at him. Ten lepers stood at a distance calling, "Jesus, Master, have pity on us!" Jesus knew exactly what they wanted.

"Go, show yourselves to the priests," He called back. They turned to do just that, and as they walked away in obedience they were healed. Jesus must have smiled as He watched each one look down at his hands and feet, his arms and legs, finding the monstrous leprosy now gone.

Whoops of joy echoed back. He saw them dance and leap and hug one another, their shouts growing fainter as they went. Turning again toward Jerusalem, Jesus resumed His journey.

Suddenly, a lone Samaritan came running back shouting, "Master, Master! Wait!" Breathless, he fell at Jesus' feet weeping and praising God, "Oh, Master! How can I thank You?" (Again, this account is from the VSV.)

"Were not all ten cleansed?" Jesus replied thoughtfully. I picture Him stroking the man's head. "Where are the other nine? Was no one found to return and give praise to God except this foreigner?"

Then, lifting him up by the hand, Jesus said, "Rise and go; your faith has made you well."

That's grace.

Father Girzone's advice, "Take no offense," takes grace indeed.

Our families alone give us lots of opportunities to practice grace. Just this morning my ninety-three-year-old mother called from the nursing home to report someone had stolen all her credit cards last night. Where were they? Did I know what happened to them?

"You no longer have credit cards, Mother," I explained. "They aren't needed in the nursing home. I'll help you buy what you need."

She needed a new outfit. Soon. She had nothing to wear.

"I'll do my best." Since Mother lives in New York, and I am in Florida, I'd have to make arrangements for someone from the nursing home to take her shopping. It wouldn't be easy on many levels. I also knew she probably wouldn't like whatever I bought. *Father, show me what to do.*

"Take no offense."

Whether it's unacknowledged gifts or a relative with frequent demands for help, giving to an ungrateful receiver isn't easy. It takes Christlike graciousness and wisdom to know when to give and when to stop.

So what did Jesus do when people weren't grateful, when they were critical of His goodness, wanting more and more, like spoiled children?

He learned to take His orders and rewards from His heavenly Father alone. God sees the gift and giver. Jesus learned to serve, as we must, expecting nothing in return. At times it was disappointing, even for Him.

I can be just as ungrateful as the nine cleansed lepers. I'm happy to have my big answer to prayer, sure, but have I thanked God enough? It's funny how quickly a tired spirit grows less thankful. When depression, fatigue, or illnesses are to blame, we need to take care of our body first. Drop back and rest. See a doctor. Do what is needed to get well again.

Expressing thanks to God daily is the first step on the road to recovery. We never run out of reasons to thank Him, for His mercies are new every morning. His love for us is certain no matter how others treat us.

When you brush up against an ungrateful world regularly

(and who doesn't?), consider what Jesus said. "Rejoice and be glad, because great is your reward in heaven, for in the same way they persecuted the prophets who were before you" (Matthew 5:12). You are in great company. God sees your heart as you serve Him alone. And all heaven is cheering you on.

Incidentally, I found an outfit for my mother that she liked. God is so good.

LIVING WATER

"If you have any encouragement from being united with Christ, if any comfort from his love, if any fellowship with the Spirit, if any tenderness and compassion, then make my joy complete by being like-minded, having the same love, being one in spirit and purpose. Do nothing out of selfish ambition or vain conceit, but in humility consider others better than yourselves."

PHILIPPIANS 2:1–3

Today's Replenishment

Mentally review a list of people who have hurt you.
Write them down in your prayer journal in pencil.
Now read Colossians 3:12–14. If your list includes
some you've not yet forgiven, this would be a good
time to do that. Ask God to show you at least one
good thing you learned from each experience. Erase
the names as you forgive them. "As far as the east is
from the west, so far has he removed our
transgressions from us" (Psalm 103:12).

You'll be amazed at what God does next. Not only
will you have gained emotional and spiritual
freedom from those hurts, but sometimes God
turns them into ministry. What a victory over evil!

Serving the ungrateful brings us closer to the heart
of God. He does it all the time. Are you
experiencing ungratefulness from someone today?
Ask God what to do. Get prayer support from
others, and Christian counseling if needed.
God will help you "take no offense."
Then you can let Him handle the rest.

8

WOULD IT BE
SO BAD TO RUN AWAY?

At the risk of belaboring my worst moments, when life's challenges lasted too long, running away had tremendous appeal. It frequently overcame me in the car. Coming home on the New York State Thruway, I'd see a sign just before my exit announcing, "Buffalo 260 miles." Oh, how I wanted to go! I could just keep driving, maybe surprise Lauren and Mike and the kids. No one would miss me for a few days. Yeah, right!

Returning home from a rare vacation was worse. As soon as the car headed toward Albany, a sense of dread crept in. How many messages would be on the answering machine from my mother? Ten? Fifteen? The record was twenty-eight. Even with daytime caregivers

in place, she would hide in her room and call me with complaints.

"She's stealing my food!"

"She said she organized my closet today and then took piles of my clothes to her car. I'm thinking of calling the police."

"My furnace is broken again."

"My wallet is missing."

"Never mind, I found it."

Some were funny, like, "My phone is broken."

As sad as it was watching Alzheimer's rob my mother of her mind, I feared I might lose my own. Steve bought me a talking phone to monitor calls. Its robotic voice punctuated the day. "Call from out of area" usually meant a telemarketer. "Call from Colonie" (where my mother lived) meant wait and listen for the message. Even with daily visits to my mother in between writing and producing my own radio show, as soon as I drove into the driveway, my phone was ringing with more requests and complaints, helpers fired, bills lost or unpaid, real or imagined emergencies. I felt trapped with no way out.

You may not face the same dilemmas I once did; yours may be far worse. I have three friends now caring for invalid husbands day and night. That's worse. Several other friends continue their speaking and writing ministries while one of their children is in prison. Carol Kent, whose heartbreaking story is told in her book *When I Lay My Isaac Down,* ministers with sacrificial love and understanding to broken people around the world. What an example she is to me! I imagine there are many days Carol would like to run away from the harsh realities she faces.

Are you ready to run screaming into the night? Before you do, try a little self-check. Ask yourself what you really need. Perhaps it's a lifestyle change, or just a weekend away. Possibly it's counseling with a pastor, a professional counselor, or a mentor to guide you through a difficult situation. Every healthy Christian finds herself in need of outside wisdom at times. Don't let pride keep you from asking for help.

Next, be brutally honest. Do you have a blind spot you're not willing to deal with? I feared one day I'd have to bring Mother to live with us. I love my mother very much and always have, but living under one roof would never work. I knew it and she did too. I finally sought counseling with a Christian counselor whose assurances with biblical boundaries changed my life and set me free from false guilt. He explained I could serve Mother with the purpose of pleasing God alone, and not try to make her happy, an impossible task.

Last, listen to your "interior monologue," the way you rehearse your problems and potential solutions to yourself. You may be living in fear of what might happen next, just like I was. Ruminating on your problems is just spinning your wheels in the sand, going nowhere but deeper into a mess.

Our fears are often counterfeit guilt trips the devil uses to keep us from fully trusting God. If you are afraid God's will is the worst thing you could imagine, follow that thought to its source. It isn't from God. His plan for you is good, as He says in Jeremiah 29:11: "'For I know the plans I have for you,' declares the LORD, 'plans to prosper you and not to harm you, plans to give you hope and a future.'" You can believe it.

Blind spots and fears are no fun to fix, but your general

health is far more important. Before you blame yourself for caving in under pressure, get a thorough physical, blood tests and all. Give someone close to you permission to ask you tough questions. Are you sleeping well, eating well? Gaining or losing weight? Irritable or frequently angry? Experiencing headaches or chest pains? Putting off caring for yourself can lead to far worse problems than you face now.

Diagnosing oneself means having a fool for a patient. Earlier in this book, I shared my initial symptoms of depression. I thought I was having an allergic reaction to food. Depression, hypertension, heart ailments, and other serious health problems often arrive disguised as things we think we can manage with a few Tums or Advil. Big mistake!

Still want to run away but can't? I know the feeling well. Here's something you can do today. And it's free.

Yes, free.

Once you've done an honest self-examination for underlying problems, consider two therapies that worked wonders for me. Now I can't imagine a day without a good dose of both: sleep and laughter.

Get a nap. Even twenty to thirty minutes daily putting your feet up will make a huge difference.

Get a great night's sleep. Begin by quieting your heart hours before bedtime with a funny movie (the more outrageous the better) or a good book (nothing heavy). Add a small snack, plus a few minutes reading the Word of God before you snuggle into bed. May I add how pleasant it is to fall asleep in a neat bedroom with clean sheets? Treat yourself like a princess at home with a pretty bedroom. Need a new mattress? Sheets and comforter? Get them. Make it your favorite room in the house. As you go to sleep, release yourself and your concerns to God in prayer. Singing a worship song in your heart is a wonderful way to do that.

It helps to limit unsettling news broadcasts and television shows during your renewal time. I'm a news addict, but I've learned to pick up the news in the morning on the Internet on the days I'm stressed or overtired. The aim is to keep your mind peaceful and at rest before sleeping. Close your eyes with a prayer of thanks to God for loving you and taking care of everything you need. Then sleep like a baby.

Laughter is my favorite medicine. I love to hang out with friends who like to laugh and have fun together. I love all my friends, but tend to walk a wider circle around those whose regular conversations pull me under when I'm paddling hard to keep my head above water. I have lots of empathy for those needing encouragement, but little tolerance, I confess, for negative people who grumble and complain.

Someone is saying, "Wait a minute! Isn't this a Christian book? What about prayer?"

Prayer is like breathing; it's our continual lifeline to God's heart. But great saints in the Bible, even God's Son, still needed to nap, fellowship, and laugh with friends. Real renewal encompasses the whole person. Every part matters.

Wanting to run away isn't sinful, but it's an alarm bell. Clearly, changes are needed. Ignoring our own needs courts disaster. With God's help, my husband's encouragement, and the prayers of many treasured friends, I'm writing this book for others needing renewal as I did. There are no shortcuts, but a friend pointing in the right direction helps.

Why not ask God for two things: a Kerith Brook place to rest very soon, and the grace to stay at your post until He provides it. In the interim, check out your health, put your feet up, turn off the phone and e-mail a little earlier in the day, and rediscover laughter and sound sleep. You're on your way!

LIVING WATER
"Search me, O God, and know my heart;
test me and know my anxious thoughts.
See if there is any offensive way in me,
and lead me in the way everlasting."

PSALM 139:23–24

Today's Replenishment

Psalm 139 meets us right where we are today. Read
it out loud. Where are you in these verses? Are you
wishing you could ride the wings of the morning
too? God's love is always near. No matter what's
happening, we know, "even there your hand will
guide me, your right hand will hold me fast" (verse
10). Think of a parent holding a small child by the
hand at a crossroads. When God holds us fast, He
is exercising His loving care.

What does this psalm tell us about God's motives?
Why doesn't He just let us go? Describe what
response God seeks in your life. Write a prayer in
your journal thanking Him for His everlasting love
and His good plans for you.

9

LORD, IT WOULD HELP IF I COULD SEE YOUR FACE

While plodding through the day during my years with a parched spirit, my first reaction when hitting a snag wasn't falling to my knees. I'd plod right out to the kitchen for a comforting snack. In a few years I gained twenty pounds, which was no comfort at all.

Stress eaters who reach for a chocolate chip cookie, a jar of peanut butter, or a handful of chips pay long term for their choices. Looking full length at myself in my undies in a dressing room mirror showed that my excess comfort had never left. It would be with me a long time unless I made big changes in the way I lived, responded to problems, and obeyed God. Connecting the dots meant looking at the whole picture of obedience as caring for my body and spirit equally. Were not both really His? When one is out of kilter, can our view of God be clear?

This summer I joined First Place (www.firstplace.org), a Christian weight loss program. It's really a life program, helping me relearn priorities I once thought were in place, but were lacking. Recording daily prayer and Bible reading, Scripture study and memorization, exercise, encouraging others, faithfulness in eating wisely, helped me see in black-and-white how lax I was in life management. Like clutter around the house, pounds around the waist are a good barometer. Am I running for comfort to food or to God?

To date I've lost seventeen pounds, walk two miles a day, love the extra Bible reading and Scripture study, and best of all, enjoy praying for the women in our on-line group who are doing the same thing.

Guess what else I'm learning? In the long run, it's easier and far better to drop to your knees. Putting God in first place means reordering life around His priorities, not using a quick fix to do what only God can do. Turning to the "snack god" yields discouragement, laziness, and spiritual sluggishness. What we really need is a clearer view of God Himself in the middle of our circumstances.

One woman in the Bible, a pregnant teenager named Mary, captured my heart with the way she embraced change and trusted God when she might easily have turned away. She was so young, yet Mary found the face of God in a spirit of submission. How rare a gem is that?

Mary may have been by the well in Nazareth when the

angel Gabriel appeared to her. There she was, probably alone, bending down to dip her water jug in the bubbling well. With one heavenly announcement, God altered her life forever. Her response changed human history.

I wonder. What was Mary thinking before the angel spoke? A virgin pledged to marry Joseph, both from respected Jewish families, I picture her humming softly, dreaming of her wedding when Gabriel interrupted her with a personal announcement from Yahweh. "Greetings, you who are highly favored! The Lord is with you" (Luke 1:28).

Luke tells us Mary was "greatly troubled." I'd have been terrified, would have dropped my water jug right there. Gabriel was quick to comfort, "Do not be afraid, Mary, you have found favor with God." Mary was speechless. The angel continued, "You will be with child and give birth to a son, and you are to give him the name Jesus. He will be great and will be called the Son of the Most High. The Lord God will give him the throne of his father David, and he will reign over the house of Jacob forever; his kingdom will never end" (Luke 1:29–33).

Mary asked simply, "How will this be, since I am a virgin?"

Gabriel explained that the Holy Spirit would come upon her and she would conceive the Son of God. "I am the Lord's servant. May it be to me as you have said."

Mission complete, Gabriel reported back to heaven. Mary lifted her head to face a life interrupted by God.

Had I been with Mary that day, once I regained my voice I'd have never stopped talking. "Mary, did you hear that? Favored by God? What did he mean by that? Joseph is history when he hears this. It'll probably kill your parents when they find out you're pregnant. Say, are you pregnant yet? Do you feel any different? Man, nobody's going to believe this!"

Rather than rush around Nazareth recounting her angel encounter, Mary packed a bag, saddled her donkey, and rode far south to the hill country of Judah to visit Elizabeth, also miraculously pregnant in her old age, with a son. She greeted Mary joyfully, "Blessed is she who has believed that what the Lord has said to her will be accomplished!" (Luke 1:45).

At that affirmation, Mary's heart erupted in a song of praise. I hope you will read Mary's Song and the magnificent events that followed in chapter 1 of Luke's gospel.

Mary remembered whose she was. She was God's child, His young woman, His servant. She didn't understand much beyond that. Rather than let her thoughts run wild with anxious questions, she disciplined them by keeping a steady focus on the God she knew to be true.

It's easy to forget God's promises when we're all wrapped up in our discomfort of the moment. Mary found joy in obeying God and accepting the circumstances He gave her. That's a challenge for most of us twice her age or more.

Mary worshiped God where she was, even though her circumstances were nothing like her former plans. Are yours? Neither are mine. But God's plans are better than any daydream I ever had. It just took me awhile to see that. How about you?

Want to see God better? Mary took her eyes off herself and looked in faith to God, choosing to worship and adore Him, praise and thank Him. Did she wonder what God was doing?

Probably, but she never wavered. And God honored her beyond her wildest dreams.

We may feel like small potatoes next to Mary, but we have the same God who still speaks to each of us personally. He has a unique and perfect plan for our lives. He rejoices over our worship, obedience, and faith, just like He did over hers. Oh, that our heart would submit like Mary's and turn for comfort to our heavenly Father!

O Lord, give me a heart like Mary's heart. Let me see Your face as I focus on who You are and not on my circumstances. Amen.

LIVING WATER
"Now the Lord is the Spirit, and where the Spirit of the Lord is, there is freedom. And we, who with unveiled faces all reflect the Lord's glory, are being transformed into His likeness with ever-increasing glory, which comes from the Lord, who is the Spirit."

2 CORINTHIANS 3:17–18

Today's Replenishment

Do you have circumstances in your life you've
never accepted? Perhaps you didn't understand
them. Who does? Relief moves in when we pray,
"May it be to me, Lord, as You will."
The struggle is gone and peace moves
in as you invite God to work.

Want to see God's face too? It will mean lifting
your eyes to Him, allowing Him to fill all your
vision. A heart fully confessed will be cleansed and
at peace with God. When the gaze of
your heart is fixed on Jesus,
life becomes a romance shared with Him.

Write out the words to your favorite hymn or
worship song. Sing it back to Jesus all day in your
heart, out loud, even while you are working, and
watch what happens. You'll begin to sense God's
presence everywhere. Looking at Him, we are
changed from the inside out.

10

IT WOULD HELP IF YOU WOULD TALK OUT LOUD

My granddaughter Jillian is almost seven. Her honey blonde hair, blue eyes, and missing front teeth are captivating, especially to this Nana. But what really makes Jillian special is her thoughtfulness. She's careful with her words, her dolls, and her tea set. She takes great pains making her second grade homework neat and correct, listens carefully to her mama and daddy and her teacher. Jillian is also thoughtful about what she believes. My daughter phoned this morning and told me Jillian has been asking how God speaks to people. Why can't she hear Him out loud?

For all of us who have Jillian's question still lurking inside, why *doesn't* God just talk out loud? It would make following Him so much easier. Knowing what to do would be a breeze! Or would it?

If Jillian were here right now, I could ask her if she always does what her mommy and daddy say. Even though she's a very good girl, she's also an honest one. Jillian would probably say, "Most of the time."

"Why only most of the time, honey? What's wrong with all the time?"

"Well, sometimes I don't want to."

"Do you ever pretend not to hear?"

"Not really, but sometimes I don't feel like listening."

Me too, honey. Me too. The fact is, sometimes I don't feel like listening to God either. I think I know what He would tell me. "Love one another as I have loved you." "Be kind and compassionate to one another, forgiving each other, just as in Christ God forgave you." Things like that.

When I don't want to hear God's voice, I get busy with important things, "spiritual things" that everyone knows take a lot of time. Before long an uncomfortable feeling sets in, gentle but urgent, like a mouse nibbling at my toes. I can't stand it until things are right again with God and me.

But first He has to get my attention. That's the challenge. In my book *Donkeys Still Talk,* based on the story of Balaam and his talking donkey in Numbers 22, I shared how God sent a "donkey" into my life about seven years ago: Bell's palsy. You can't be a speaker and have half your face paralyzed at the beginning of your speaking season without realizing God is trying to get your attention, and He has something very important to say! My schedule came to a halt until I got the message.

Busyness provides a believable cover-up for a dried-up spirit or a strong will. I've met women at conferences who confessed their unwillingness to do what God wanted if it wasn't what they thought best.

"Oh, I can't believe God would ask that of me. I'm certain my ministry is His will. I'll get through this."

"My husband's the one who needs changing. He's the problem here, not me."

"I'm the only person who can do this. I can't stop now."

Imagine that? Pride takes root in all our arguments with God.

To hear God's voice, I must want to. I mean *want to*. It's not optional, like breakfast. I also need a listening place where I'm quiet enough and alone enough to hear Him. When we live on every word that comes from His mouth, that means eating up God's Word like the daily Bread it is. And why wouldn't we? It's fresh baked daily just for us. Open your Bible and Jesus brings the meal!

Our family doctor admits he has a little weight problem. But then, who wouldn't when his family owns the largest Italian bakery in the area? Every morning before dawn a delivery truck brings him fresh hot bread and Italian rolls right to his front door. He wouldn't think of not eating them. Neither would I. Imagine smelling the aroma waiting for you every day in God's Word. Fresh words just for you. Rise and eat, child. You look hungry.

God also speaks through people He sends with a message. Often they are just regular people, not necessarily Christians, who don't even know their significance at the time. But their words hit like a zinger in your soul. Has that happened to you?

Perhaps you've been the "zinger-bearer" and were shocked to learn how your casual message met someone's aching need at the time. As Jillian's baby sister Kerith says, "Great job, you!"

The most intimate way God speaks to His children is through the inner whispers of the Holy Spirit living in you. Amazing grace! How sweet the sound of God's gentle urging, His caution right when you need it, His tender word of comfort. Is anything more wonderful than God's personal words whispered to your soul?

This is not just a once-in-a-lifetime occurrence. Not at all. God speaks a stream of thoughts to us all day long, even at night while we are sleeping. Psalm 139 affirms this in verses 17 and 18. "How precious to me are your thoughts, O God! How vast is the sum of them! Were I to count them, they would outnumber the grains of sand. When I awake, I am still with you."

I want to tell Jillian tonight that God speaks best to children. In fact, He wants us to become like children when we approach Him. Perhaps it's because they listen best, all snuggled up on His lap with their honest questions, their longing to make sense out of the world, to be known and loved. He told His disciples, "I tell you the truth, unless you change and become like little children, you will never enter the kingdom of heaven. Therefore, whoever humbles himself like this child is the greatest in the kingdom of heaven" (Matthew 18:3–4).

Imagine yourself as a child on Jesus' lap right now. Lean back on His shoulder and feel His heartbeat and the gentle vibrations from His voice. Look around at all He has made: the sky, the trees, animals, flowers, and you. What's He saying?

His children listen best and eat up every word. When you're ready, tell Him what you need. He's ready to answer.

LIVING WATER

"My sheep listen to my voice; I know them, and they follow me. I give them eternal life, and they shall never perish; no one can snatch them out of my hand."

JOHN 10:27–28

Today's Replenishment

■

Of all the reasons to keep a journal, none is more
valuable over time than recording the words God
speaks to you. It may be through a special verse like
today's "Living Water." An elderly Persian
Christian, Sam Sade, prayed for me to know Jesus
from the time I was seven until I became a
Christian at twenty-five. He was the first person I
called with the news. Soon a letter arrived from
Sam affirming his joy over God's faithfulness. He
included this verse in John 10. I wrote it down in
my first journal and memorized it.

I wish I had always done that over the years. I try to
be more faithful now at recording what God is
saying to me through His Word, the inner voice of
the Holy Spirit, the trend of circumstances He
allows, and other people. Why not do the same?
Nothing is more encouraging when you are feeling
exhausted, depressed, or just dull than reviewing
personal words God has spoken to you.
Don't miss it.

11

COULD YOU ANSWER MY PRAYERS A LITTLE SOONER?

I wait much better at the dentist when she says, "Just a few more minutes and we're done." But God doesn't say that. He says, "Wait. Sit still." Just like my father did when I was a girl. After a long walk in dark times, knowing the tunnel is about to end would help. Relief came as a total surprise.

Late one December afternoon, I stopped at the supermarket after the holiday crowd left our house. Minus numbers on the thermometer reminded me a long winter lay ahead for the Northeast. After taking a meal to my mother, listening to her caregiver's whispered complaints, and wondering what to do next, it felt good to be alone in the warm store. It was surprisingly empty. Turning off my cell phone, I

walked slowly up and down the aisles gathering my thoughts. Amy was at last independent, but Mother's tether grew tighter every day. What if the caregiving never ended? What if she outlived me? Who would take care of her then?

Mechanically tossing groceries into the cart, I wiped away tears and groaned a prayer for wisdom and strength. It didn't matter who saw me. *O God, I just don't know what to do anymore. Please help me. Please show the way. I can't keep going much longer.*

About half an hour later, the car loaded, I sat at a red light. The clock on the dash glowed exactly 5:00. Suddenly, I cried out, "Lord, please take this from me!" I had no idea God would answer so fast.

Steve met me at the door with a quick kiss. The phone was ringing. "I'll get the groceries while you answer that."

"Call from Colonie," the phone announced. It was Mother. I heard panic in her voice. "I can't move."

"What's wrong?"

"I don't know. I just can't move."

"Where are you?"

"On my bed."

"Can I talk with Darla a minute?"

"I sent her home. I called the neighbors."

"We'll be right over. Don't worry."

Steve and I jumped back in the car for the fifteen-minute drive to her home. He did it in twelve. Halfway there, I called 911 and asked them to meet us at the house.

The ambulance arrived about the same time we did.

Mother sat rigidly in her favorite chair wearing a dirty night-gown I had never seen before.

"How did you get to your chair?"

"Oh, they moved me."

"The neighbors?" How, I wondered? It troubled me that they moved her and then left. What if she was having a stroke?

The gentle ambulance attendants took over as we watched, offering words of assurance as they carried her out sitting bolt upright on a stretcher.

Instantly life changed. Mother was hospitalized about a week for evaluation. A team of specialists examined her, questioned us all, ordered multiple tests, and determined she had suffered a mild heart episode and had progressive dementia, probably Alzheimer's. The larger problem was her safety living alone. Their conclusions, clearer and more definitive than my own, were made. Legally the hospital could not release her into an unsafe environment. They ordered twenty-four-hour care in her home under their supervision until a bed in a nursing home was available. Mother was mad. Fighting mad. But I was free for the first time in years.

It felt almost ethereal. Others were in charge now, people other than me. A fresh parade of competent professionals she couldn't fire took over her medications, her physical needs, her protests. These angelic beings arranged for in-home caregivers who arrived like clockwork, each with a special skill. Oh, the joy of it! The peace! But soon, the guilt.

Others had held on longer than I, changing adult diapers (I never had to do that, thank God), lugging wheelchairs, combing hair and brushing the teeth of those who once made their birthday cakes or carried them over the threshold. Why had I not been stronger? But this was not my doing, I reminded myself. God had taken over for me and set me free.

Relief soon trickled back, then fell in torrents, leaving me drenched in thanksgiving. It hardly mattered now, but I still wondered, *Why so long a wait, God?*

Others came to mind. Hannah's long-term wait for a son consumed her. She agonized with God, casting her sorrow in His hands. God answered her prayer when hope had dried up like her womb. Her child Samuel would anoint kings.

Abraham and Sarah waited for God to fulfill His promise of offspring outnumbering the sand. Nothing happened but Ishmael, an arranged son of sorrow born to Hagar, Sarah's servant. Isaac, the promised son, would come years later.

Elizabeth received her miracle boy, John, in her later years. He would announce the Christ. The Shunnamite woman waited long years for a child, only to have him die in her arms. Where was God? Elijah's prayers breathed life back into her boy. Why these long waits? What was God saying in my own small story?

Perhaps the extended wait births the story. Those who learn to sit still and wait have something amazing worth telling. God answered my prayer! God did this. Not me! I tried and couldn't. He lifted my burdens when I could no longer bear them. Has God given you a job after waiting a long time? Has He brought a prodigal home, released someone you love from addiction, or saved an unbelieving spouse?

Or not. You may still be waiting. Will God answer? Yes, He will. Soon? I pray so. He may not answer as you expect, or even as you hope, but His answer will be best. And He is near. All the time.

LIVING WATER

*"I waited patiently for the LORD; he
turned to me and heard my cry. He lifted
me out of the slimy pit, out of the mud and
mire; he set my feet on a rock and gave me
a firm place to stand. He put a new song
in my mouth, a hymn of praise to our God.
Many will see and fear and
put their trust in the LORD."*

PSALM 40:1–3

Today's Replenishment

What long-term answers to prayer are you waiting for today? Most of us have more than one. I'm sure you have already listed them in your prayer journal, but if not, why not do so today? Write out a prayer to God telling Him how you feel, what your fears are, and what you would most love for Him to do. Then thank Him now for His best will in each of these needs. Thank Him for answering your prayer even if you don't get to see it. Thank Him by faith. Begin today saying, "Thank You, Lord. May Your will be done" in each situation. The peace will come. So will your answer.

The verses above are my "life verses." Do you have a life verse, one that symbolizes what God has done for you? If you do, write it in the front of your Bible and memorize it. Claim the promise God has given you specifically. If you don't have one, ask God for it. He loves to oblige His children and lavish His goodness all over their lives.

12

I WANT YOUR WILL, BUT I'M AFRAID

To be honest, living with God's answers to prayer can be scary. Our new lifestyle and Mother's required big adjustments. She found it difficult not to be in control, the very reason I felt such relief. Her phone calls reflected her frustration.

"The physical therapist just came. I'm exhausted now from using the walker."

"The nurse did my pills. I think she did them all wrong."

"They're here too often. I can't get any peace and quiet."

"How soon are you coming over? I need a few things at the store."

"I don't want these people coming here anymore."

Though I still visited often, I was no longer in charge. Hallelujah! With 24/7 care we were suddenly able to drive to Florida for a three-week vacation planned a year before. I hardly dared to leave, but Steve insisted, "Others can take over now. You and I need a good rest." Agreed.

Rest we did. Once we unpacked at Disney's Vero Beach Resort, we sat by the pool and read a stack of Agatha Christie mysteries, walked the beach, ate great meals while overlooking the ocean, and rediscovered laughter and romance in a spectacular setting. Three weeks there wasn't enough. On our last day in Florida, Steve said brightly, "Hey, why not stop at this realty office and see how much condos cost?" It was totally unlike my conservative husband.

"Why would we do that?"

"I don't know. Just for fun, check out their brochures. I'll wait in the car."

Half an hour later, Steve came into the office, a temporary trailer set up after the recent hurricanes. I was seated at the computer having a lively conversation with a real-estate agent. Nothing I love like looking at houses!

"I think I'm in trouble now," Steve said, but he smiled and sat down to have a look with us.

"Nothing available right now but two hurricane-damaged condos," she said. "Beautiful location near here. Want to have a look?"

"Why not?" we both agreed. It was five minutes' drive from the beach and our hotel to a magical resort community of lakes, fountains, tennis courts, a golf course, and a marina. The whole place beckoned strongly to Steve. The newer condo was trashed. One look and I nixed the idea in favor of the less damaged and more expensive one for sale.

We took a leap and put in a bid, far lower than the price. It was quickly turned down. "Oh, well, I guess that's it," we said, and packed to leave for home the next morning. We stopped at Hilton Head to catch up with a dear friend before we left, and my cell phone rang while we walked on the beach together. It was the real-estate agent. Did we want to put in a bid on the totally trashed condo? The association would repair it at their own expense except for cosmetics like paint and flooring. Knowing Steve's feelings and mine were alike, I thought *Why not?* I made an offer over the phone while Steve and our friend Norma walked on the beach about fifty paces ahead of me.

What seemed like minutes later, the agent called again. The seller wanted only a little more to close the deal. Would we do it? Steve and Norma weren't within earshot. Since it was beginning to feel like Monopoly money now, I said, "Sure. That's fine." When I caught up with Steve, I told him what I'd done. "Oh, the realtor called and I said go ahead and put in a little higher offer. I may have just bought the condo."

He smiled like the Cheshire cat, like he knew all along it would happen. Norma cheered. We were euphoric.

Reality set in a couple of days later as we headed north again. Now what?

"I say we fix it up for one day in the future," I suggested. "We could rent it out until then."

"It'll take time and be expensive." Steve was back in his cautious mode.

Ever the Pollyanna, I added, "We could do it a little at a

time. Go down whenever we can and work on it." Seemed like a good idea to me. We tossed ideas back and forth all the way up I-95.

Just as we passed the "Welcome to Virginia" sign, Steve turned to me with resolve and said, "I don't want to do that."

"But we've already put money down. . . ."

"No, I want to live there."

"Live there? Like all the time? What would we do with our house?"

Steve was already retired, and I could write and speak from Florida just as well. But moving had never once occurred to me. All I could think was, *Mother will kill me.*

"We'll sell the house! Start over! It'll be fun, a great new adventure. We've talked about it for years, why not do it? You're not needed anymore. We'll be there every summer and you can visit during the year all you like." But I knew talking about it and doing it were two different things. This would take serious grace. Bold grace.

At home Mother was busy making her own plans. The best nursing home in the area notified her that a room was available. We had anticipated many months' wait. Suddenly, she was in. And miracle of miracles, Mother had grown tired of the parade of caregivers in and out of her home and was more than willing to move. It had to be God!

Still, the sudden change scared me. I felt like Sarai when Abram (later Sarah and Abraham) announced they'd be leaving their homeland and moving somewhere far away. Where? God would tell them where. Why? Just because God said so. How did she feel being married to this visionary spirit? We learned at the British Museum that Ur was not just a bunch of tents. It was the New York City of the ancient world. Abram left behind not only deep roots but also a sophisticated, highly developed, and educated culture. It wasn't easy packing up their life, loading everything on camels and wagons and setting out for a hidden land far beyond the Euphrates. Could I do something like that? Yes, perhaps I could. In fact, I would. It began to feel right in every way.

Miracles tend to cluster in bunches. Every step of our path was strewn with them. A Christian family bought our house six days after we put it on the market. They had prayed long and hard and knew it was the right one. A perfect fit. Steve and I giggled as their kids squealed with joy walking through the newly decorated bedrooms and saw their new backyard. Gracious people, solid in their faith. How good is God?

Mother insisted her house be sold at the same time. In six weeks we cleaned and packed it up. It also sold in six days, but that's a story for another day.

Now I am convinced beyond doubt that God loves to surprise us with His will, which is always worth waiting for. His plans, no matter how trying, are always good. And His path always leads us home.

LIVING WATER

"Delight yourself in the LORD and he will give you the desires of your heart. . . .
If the LORD delights in a man's way,
he makes his steps firm; though he stumble,
he will not fall, for the LORD upholds
him with his hand."

PSALM 37:4, 23–24

Today's Replenishment

Patience in trials is the rub. James exhorts,
"Consider it pure joy, my brothers and sisters,
whenever you face trials of many kinds, because
you know that the testing of your faith produces
perseverance. Let perseverance finish its work
so that you may be mature and complete,
not lacking anything" (James 1:2–4 TNIV).

During the caregiver years I was a long way from
seeing things like James did. I wanted to. Very
badly. But the reality was, it was a daily struggle on
my knees begging God for grace to get me through
each day. Some days were easier than others, but
not many. I lacked long-term patience and
perseverance, something that comes by inches
when you're busy doing the next thing.

Are you lacking in patience too? It helps to know
that God is aiming at something very good. Peter
underlines this with his words "In this you greatly
rejoice, though now for a little while you may have
had to suffer grief in all kinds of trials. These have
come so that your faith—of greater worth than
gold, which perishes even though refined by fire—
may be proved genuine and may result in praise,
glory and honor when Jesus Christ is revealed"
(1 Peter 1:6–7). Hang in there, dear friend.
Help is around the corner.

13

SQUEEZE MY HAND
ONE MORE TIME, LORD

Relocating far from home and family is a sobering thought. Naturally, most of our friends thought we weren't serious, or were just a little off. "Do you mean move, as in leave the area entirely? Why would you do that?"

"What about your home? You've raised your kids there. Are they okay with this idea?"

One close friend was even angry. We began to feel like college kids announcing we were hitchhiking around the country for the summer.

Our kids took a parental tone. "It's not that we are against this idea, but have you considered where you want to be in five years?"

"You'll be far away from family if health problems occur."

"How expensive will this be, anyway? Can you afford it?"

But, in the end, the kids seemed genuinely happy for us.

Our friends' comments eventually morphed into "I wish we could do the same thing."

"You're smart to take a leap when you're still young enough to enjoy it."

"Hey, why not? Go for it!"

Then we looked at the garage. Crammed. And our closets. Too much stuff. Under the beds. Yup. More stuff. Everywhere we looked, thirty-one years of memorabilia stared back. Staggered by the amount of sorting and hoeing out involved, I said, "Are we crazy? What about you? Are you still sure about this?"

"I am."

"Me too."

Just to be sure God hadn't changed His mind, we prayed again and asked God to make it abundantly clear. *Just close the door, Lord, if we've made a huge mistake.*

The house sold instantly. The questions stopped. Strangely, even Mother, who always loved real estate, was happy for us. When we finished dismantling, we promised ourselves a party.

Energy is at least doubled by hope and cheerfulness. Steve and I tackled the house room by room, stopping often to share memories or a good laugh. I expected to cry as we unearthed family treasures, and sometimes we both did. Mostly, we listened to praise music or oldies rock and roll while we worked, bought fast food with two-for-one coupons at night, and took loads of junk to the trash. The days clipped by, awash with joy.

After a period of adversity, it's easy to forget how good

hope feels. The past eight or nine years weighed heavily, carrying us slowly uphill to some veiled goal. I'd missed a lot of God's fingerprints all over my life. How sad.

Reading in the book of Colossians one day, these verses called my name:

> Let the peace of Christ rule in your hearts, since as members of one body you were called to peace. And be thankful. Let the word of Christ dwell in you richly as you teach and admonish one another with all wisdom, and as you sing psalms, hymns and spiritual songs with gratitude in your hearts to God. And whatever you do, whether in word or deed, do it all in the name of the Lord Jesus, giving thanks to God the Father through Him. (Colossians 3:15–17)

Apparently, I had lost the vision, and my song, as well. Instead of thankfulness, psalms, and hymns of praise, an inner posture of stoicism silently took up residence, and along with it, stagnation I couldn't detect. What a sorry state.

Knowing all too well the only way to fix a messed-up soul was through confession, I prayed. *O God, cleanse me from this sinful waste of my life. Forgive me for looking to my circumstances for satisfaction instead of to You! Teach me to be thankful again, to rejoice in who You are, and to sing Your praises again. Help me back onto the path of faith.*

I marveled at my husband, Steve. After he had come through several long years of discouragement at his job, two years earlier God opened the door for early retirement and a meaningful ministry. Long before the opportunity for release came, Steve began listening daily to Christian radio to and from work, and on earphones whenever it was appropriate at his desk. Over time, his spirit bloomed again. Steve was back! He spread a lovely aroma of Christ everywhere he went.

That's what I needed: a complete overhaul. Nothing less would do. I asked God to renew my spirit one room at a time. Cleaning our own house became a daily metaphor of the liberation my soul needed. I praised God on my knees or on a ladder every day. In time, a cheerful heart lifted me once again.

Steve and I were on a roll. We celebrated answers to prayer hourly. The movers gave us a huge discount for signing a contract in early spring. The condo association in Florida put our trashed unit on the front burner, hastening the repairs so we could move in. Not until we arrived in Florida did we realize others had put their own repairs on hold, and handled lots of legwork, so ours could get done. In Albany our wonderful real-estate agent, a close friend, gave us a discount for listing my mother's house as well. He also found a reliable worker to bring her once beautiful home up to saleable condition. The list goes on. In the midst of this, one day I realized how happy I'd become. No more stoicism or complaining. God was wowing us as our dream unfolded daily.

Are you like I was? Have you forgotten that God gives good gifts to His children, including you? Not finding much reason to celebrate? I might have shortened my recovery time had I remembered two things: pray far more expectantly, watching for God's answers; and be ready to obey Him quickly, no matter what He says. No backpedaling or second-guessing.

Just do it. A party is on the way and quite possibly a new dream.

Feel like you don't deserve God's surprises? None of us does. When God gives you a gift that's over the top, bigger than you ever thought possible, accept it with grace and thanksgiving. He already gave us eternal life, bought at the cross with His Son's blood. "He who did not spare his own Son, but gave him up for us all—how will he not also, along with him, graciously give us all things?" (Romans 8:32). And when He says, "Wait, child; just a little longer," there's a very good reason why.

LIVING WATER

*"You turned my wailing into dancing;
you removed my sackcloth and clothed me
with joy, that my heart may sing to you
and not be silent. O LORD my God,
I will give you thanks forever."*

PSALM 30:11–12

Today's Replenishment

Think for a moment how the disciples felt after Jesus' crucifixion. Their dreams died with their Hero. Where could they turn now? Fishing again, tax collecting, or whatever? Things looked pretty hopeless. Don't you wish you could grab them by the shoulders and yell, "Just wait! Sunday morning's coming!" Jesus was about to revolutionize the world through them. But they could only see that day.

You and I are like that. We see today and worry tomorrow will be worse. On our best days, we are hopeful God has heard our prayers. Maybe He'll even answer one day. Not much dynamite in that faith, is there? A lot of spiritual fuzziness is cleared up by simple obedience. Ask God if there is anything you've not obeyed that He's asked of you. If something specific comes to mind, make it right. Obey with abandon and watch the light on your path steadily brighten.

14

TREASURE HUNT

I don't believe it!" Steve called down from the attic over our garage. "There's a box of rocks up here! Somebody in our family saved a box of rocks! Now I've seen everything."

"Who would do that?"

"Bobby, maybe? He always loved rocks."

"Are they pretty ones?"

"Nope. Just plain old rocks."

I could have saved them. I love rocks. "What else is up there?"

His muffled voice came down from a stuffy corner high above me. "Old pieces of carpeting, computer boxes, Christmas decorations, suitcases I haven't seen in twenty years, you name it. This box looks like old artwork the kids did in school."

"Oh, don't throw that out! I want it!"

"What are we going to do with it?"

"I'll save it and give it to our kids."

"So they can put it in their attics?"

"Of course."

Treasures long missing crept out of corners, peeked out from behind sets of dishes in the mudroom closet, appeared in forgotten dresser drawers. I set them in the growing "undecided" pile on the dining room table along with Steve's collection of Kennedy half-dollars, my grandmother's silver butter knife with the broken handle, and a tea set we bought in San Francisco's Japanese Tea Garden in 1977. What to keep, what to give to the kids, what to sell, and (gasp!) what to throw away? We needed some criteria to help us decide.

"How about keeping everything that's really sentimental? That's all the kid's artwork, all our family pictures, most of the artwork in our house."

"The books. What about the books?" Steve looked impatient already.

"Oh, well, let's take only the important ones." Hundreds of volumes filled our home. Important ones?

"I say we get rid of all our furniture too."

"You mean the family antiques? I'm sure the kids will want those. And the new family room couch. Someone will want that, I'm sure."

But they didn't. We not only asked, I tried to persuade them. Our kids already had lots of their own stuff. They only wanted a few things. The rest didn't seem to matter. Imagine that.

On a long weekend in late winter, we invited all four of

our kids and their spouses, minus grandkids. "Take anything you want!" we said. We would choose our treasures later. It was the party we'd dreamed of. They began in the garage. Out went all of Steve's tools. Where would we put them in our condo, anyway? Next, someone took the lawnmower, our garden chairs, car stuff, and some old tires. They loaded up their cars happily with much of our garage junk, something I never expected. Next, I put their childhood artwork on the dining room table and called everyone into the house. Whoops of laughter brought back celebrations from years ago. Had we enjoyed it as much then? I hope so.

"Oh, I'd forgotten painting this owl!"

"Hey, this is pretty cool! Can I have this?"

"My horse picture! And here's the deer too!"

"I won a prize for this drawing."

Lauren said it best. "This is so much fun! And just think, nobody died!"

Moving from room to room each of our children thoughtfully chose his share of family treasures The Grandma Moses print over the couch went to Amy; my uncle Jerry's painting went to Lauren, as did my bedroom quilt and matching Monet print of pink and red peonies. My daughters-in-law chose pieces of china, old silverware I'd been given by my aunt. I couldn't believe no one wanted the goblets. David took the antique wingback chair and, later, Grammy's camelback sofa.

But Bob ended up with the one thing everyone really wanted: a stack of cardboard backs from Steve's yellow legal pads on which he'd dreamed up creative family devotions over twenty years. They were classics now.

"Listen, I've got three boys and I need these more than anyone," Bob said.

"Promise you'll make copies or share them around the family," Lauren said using her "oldest sibling" voice. "Everyone's going to want a set, you know."

David arrived home just after the cardboard devotions had moved to Bob's pile, and to this day, he's still trying to get them back. Treasures take surprising forms.

It was a joyful time sorting, giving, remembering, praying together one more time around the maple dining room table I'd had all my life. Could I let go of these things and the memories they represented?

I could and I did. So did Steve. Admittedly, it hurt a bit, but it was far easier than we expected. We knew God had a new life planned for us in Florida.

We both discovered long ago that people and memories go on forever. Houses and things do not. Whether we are in Florida, or visiting our children at their homes in New York or North Carolina, our shared lives frame our memories and cast them in a light that will last forever. God is forever; people are forever; faith, hope, and love are forever. That's what we get to keep. Everything else will be left behind.

This past year Steve and I mourned the loss of four dear friends including one family member. In each case, death came unexpectedly early. Thankfully, their lives were in order. Their names were written in the Book of Life. They were ready to move Home.

How about you? Are you ready? Do you want to be?

For starters, keep in mind that God looks at life entirely

opposite of the way we do. He points the way Home, telling us to "fix our eyes not on what is seen, but on what is unseen. For what is seen is temporary, but what is unseen is eternal" (2 Corinthians 4:18). That means it's wise to hold everything visible with an open hand. Better yet, give it to God. Then one day when you must leave it, your treasure is safe with Him.

Instead, cling to the invisible, to the salvation Jesus purchased for you on the Cross when He died a cruel death to pay for your sin and mine. Cling to the promises of God that are able to take you through any trial on earth. Cling to the love of God poured into your heart through His Holy Spirit when you invited Christ into your life and were born anew into His family forever. It's the greatest treasure you will ever receive. And no one can take it away.

LIVING WATER

"Do not store up for yourselves treasures
on earth, where moth and rust destroy,
and where thieves break in and steal. But
store up for yourselves treasures in heaven,
where moth and rust do not destroy, and
where thieves do not break in and steal.
For where your treasure is, there your
heart will be also."

MATTHEW 6:19–21

Today's Replenishment

■

Insurance companies tell us to make a video recording of our valuables in case of a fire. Those things represent a large investment that will need to be replaced. What is on your treasure list today? Make a list in your journal of everything visible in your home you wouldn't want to leave behind. What gives each thing value to you?

Now make a list of invisible treasures. Those are priceless. We know nothing can ever replace what matters most in this life and for eternity. If God calls you Home any time soon, what will you take with you? What will you keep forever?

Knowing which treasures last forever and which do not, how will this affect the way you live now? What needs to change? Write it down in your journal and ask God to help you do that.

15

I Feel Like a Miracle
in Slow Motion!

If you're over thirty-five or forty, you may remember the television commercial with a couple running open-armed toward each other in slow motion through a golden field of waving grain. Our family laughed every time we saw it, imagining them either colliding or missing each other entirely. In silly moments, Steve and I still imitate them.

Extended periods of stress can end in slow motion. One by one the pressures release their grip. You can breathe normally again. Freedom seeps back by small degrees. But will it last? It seems too good to be true.

Gradually our prayers got bolder, spawning a giddy new faith. A miracle began to unfold, a God story that left us breathless. I wondered why God was showering us with all these blessings. Why now?

I found that most God stories begin with a long wait in dark times, or a crushing sorrow that casts doubt on the character of God, often becoming the story that frames your faith. It was for Ruth and Naomi, a Moabite widow and her beloved Hebrew mother-in-law.

These two shared a legendary bond. Along with Orpah, Naomi's other daughter-in-law, they grieved the losses of their men, and buried them in Moab. When Naomi urged "her girls" to go back to their Moabite families and find new husbands, Orpah left with her blessing, but Ruth would have none of it. "Where you go I will go, and where you stay I will stay. Your people will be my people and your God my God" (Ruth 1:16). Together they trudged back to Bethlehem. It was harvest time, and a slow-motion miracle had already begun.

Miracles require bold faith, a submissive spirit, and honest prayer. Between Ruth and Naomi, they had it all. For those curious whether God loves a good romance, or celebrates womanhood, or delights in surprising His children enough to make their toes tingle, read the little book of Ruth. You'll find a new wrinkle to the creative love of God. For our purposes today, I'll cut to the grand finale. It's my favorite part.

Ruth, being the loving daughter-in-law she was, followed everything Naomi suggested. As a result, she received her wealthy, godly new husband, Boaz, with the blessing of the whole town and its elders. Boaz was blown away by her character, love for Naomi, and beauty. (She *had* to be beautiful, don't you think? And Boaz, *I'm certain*, was a handsome figure too.)

Instantly it seemed, God filled her womb with a baby boy, Obed, the joy of Naomi's heart. He later fathered Jesse, whose youngest boy was a shepherd named David. How cool was that?

Get the picture? God is way ahead of us and He's making plans. Imagine His grief when we don't ask boldly, trust completely, and submit to His perfect will.

When Naomi submitted her sorrow to God and trusted Him with her future, she ended up blessing the world. In turn, she received a godly family heritage through her daughter-in-law Ruth's love and obedient faith. Aren't you glad these two women are in your spiritual ancestor bank?

One question: Whose future hangs on your obedient faith today? You can be sure someone's does. Your story is way bigger than you know.

My slow-motion miracle began with a bold but honest prayer on a frigid December night. When God answered by relieving me instantly of my mother's full-time care, I was free to rest for the first time in years. Even leaving for a few weeks' vacation was a struggle. Having managed things for so long, I wondered how it would go without me. Ha! What a foolish, prideful thought.

Once in Florida, refreshment washed over our spirits like the nearby waves. This had to be a charmed vacation. It never rained once in Florida, but our home area was featured on CNN with record snowfall. God had good plans, mind-blowing plans I would never have imagined.

Had you asked me by the pool if I'd like to live there, I'd have laughed and said, "Of course. But it's not going to happen." If someone had suggested that Steve and I purchase a condo, sell our house, and move in to Florida in three months, we'd have howled and said, "Dream on." But if someone had asked if we believed Jeremiah 29:11 where God says, "For I know the plans I have for you . . . plans to prosper you and not to harm you, plans to give you hope and a future," we'd have quickly affirmed, "Absolutely!"

Do you have difficulty believing God has good plans for you too? For you personally? Try this: Pray honestly, trust boldly, and live ready to obey the next prompting of the Holy Spirit. I might add, brace yourself. This may be a great ride.

In retrospect, our slow-motion miracle happened faster than we ever imagined, faster than anyone around us believed, but slow enough to see God's hand in it all. It's convinced me forever that God loves to wow His children with good and perfect gifts: miracle healings, miracle husbands, miracle babies, miracle jobs, miracle homes, miracle conversions, miracle joy even in the midst of sorrow. And when He seems silent or just plain slow? Wait. God's character and love never change. He's way ahead of us.

LIVING WATER
"In my anguish I cried to the LORD, and he answered by setting me free."

PSALM 118:5

Today's Replenishment

■

Can you picture Ruth and Naomi before their trip
to Bethlehem? They'd lost their dreams, were spent
with sorrow, and no doubt wept together on their
humbling trip home. I can relate. How about you?
Are you there now?

But God was at work, something we often forget.

The people of Bethlehem welcomed them with
arms of love. Naomi was their flesh and blood!
They listened to her story of loss, prayed for both
women, took them in, and cared for them. The
word spread at the city gate that two women of
faith, a widow and her daughter-in-law, had arrived
back home. Boaz was listening.

Do you think that for one moment Naomi or Ruth
imagined the magnitude of what God had
planned? God deals in big plans that stretch across
eternity. Only when Christ returns and takes us to
heaven will we comprehend the fullness of God's
glory and His will. But for now, He asks us to trust
Him at the corners of the way. He's leading us on a
new path, one we can't imagine.

Will you thank God for that? Will you write out a
bold prayer asking for faith to follow Him, inviting
God to give you new dreams, hope and a future
only He can see?

16

LIFE TRICKLES
BACK INTO MY BONES

One blistering June following Steve's grad school
years, we moved to Baltimore just in time for the
seventeen-year cicadas—large insects that emerge
every seventeen years for a month. For this bug-
fearing woman, they were my worst nightmare.
The heavy air zinged with their supremacy from
morning until night. No one was safe. Stepping
outside meant running wildly, ducking and
screaming, as locusts dive-bombed from every direction. Only the birds loved them, snapping up
an instant picnic in midair. Locust carcasses littered the walk, porch, yard, even our hair, all
summer. Recognizing their hated electric
song still puts me on alert.

But one good thing came of it.

Now I have a picture of the grand reception the prophet Joel must have received when he relayed God's message, "I will repay you for the years the locusts have eaten" (Joel 2:25). Hurray, God! We aren't dead yet.

God is giving back what was eaten up.

I wondered, just what had the locusts eaten over the previous years in my life? A lot. They'd gobbled up most of my peace; that was certain. Worry now pecked at my thought life, leaving love and patience dangling on a limb. I'd become a serious sort, prone to tears over small things, a joyless carcass of the person I'd once been. Sadly, it had begun to feel normal.

Yes, the locusts had eaten a lot. They'd also taken a big bite out of my confidence in God. I wasn't so sure anymore that He had my best interests in mind. I felt apprehensive over what He might allow next.

We all have locust seasons in life that leave us stripped mentally, spiritually, and emotionally. Whether the locusts attack our health, finances, job, or family relationships, the result is the same. When the cloud finally leaves, little remains. Only God's restoration will do. I needed it badly.

But the locusts had taken a toll on more than just me. I knew there'd be a reckoning involved. A small pile of hurts and misunderstandings within the family begged housecleaning. Preempted by more pressing needs, the camaraderie we'd once enjoyed had suffered battle fatigue. It was time to seek reconciliation. And we did. It took time mending fences, asking forgiveness, accepting one another as flawed but loved human beings. Grace won, as it always does. Hallelujah!

I'm here to tell you wonderful news. The locusts move on

when God moves in. And when God restores, He restores big time, way beyond our dreams. Without a parade of crises marching through our life, our marriage bloomed again.

Steve and I discovered some of the freshness we'd missed: daily time to unwind without fear of what might happen next, regular fellowship with friends, conversations that weren't centered on our problems for a change, freedom to make spontaneous plans, the sound of laughter at home, fewer distractions in work and ministry, and time to be a couple alone again. And a cherished connection developed with others who were suffering. We knew how to pray for them.

Seasons of sorrow will come. Exhaustion will come, and our fruitful life may seem to dry up and blow away. But it won't. My confidence in God has zoomed tenfold now. When locusts devour, God calls it pruning, and He doubles the fruit we once had.

Not too sure? Just look at Job, at one time "the greatest man among all the people of the East" (Job 1:3). When God looked at Job, he saw a man who was "blameless and upright, a man who fears God and shuns evil" (verse 8). Satan wanted him. Badly. But God had confidence Job would hold fast to his faith no matter what Satan did to him. To prove it, Satan was allowed to machine-gun all Job held dear, including his children. All but his wife. Her parroted refrain, "Curse God and die!" was a daily jab in his soul (Job 2:9).

Job pondered his plight while he sat in the dust and picked at his sores. *Why all this pain, God? Why?* And yet, he managed to keep trusting God. "Job did not sin in what he said" (Job 2:10).

That wasn't all his suffering. A visitation team was on the way. Job's three friends arrived to offer comfort. For one week they did a good job of keeping quiet and sharing his solitude, but soon they ended up blaming Job for his problems, certain that God was punishing him for sin.

Have you had people put a false face on God too? Nothing angers God more than being misrepresented by religious types who ought to know better. What scares me most is knowing how easy it is to be like them, interpreting God's actions wrongly to others. Who would have guessed that God was proving the faithfulness of Job to all of heaven? How can we know His purpose in our suffering, or another's, either? We can't.

What we do know from Scripture is that God wasn't punishing Job at all. Quite the contrary, He loved Job, trusted him, even held him up as a heavenly example of righteous living. But He never told Job why. Instead, God chastised him at length for questioning His character, thundering, "Who is this that darkens my counsel with words without knowledge?" (Job 38:2).

Job, facedown in the dirt, groveled, "My ears had heard of you but now my eyes have seen you. Therefore I despise myself and repent in dust and ashes" (Job 42:5–6).

Finally, God's anger burned at Job's friends, and He directed Job to pray for them so they might be forgiven. God then restored Job to double the prosperity he formerly enjoyed, even giving him a beautiful new family. Unfortunately, he had to keep the same wife.

Job's locust season was worse than anyone's, certainly

mine. Yet God was never far from his chaotic life, even though it seemed so. Neither was it without purpose. And the way He restored Job blows me away.

I wonder how all this affected Job's faith, his family, and his purpose in living? I can picture him saying, "I'm really living now! I'll never doubt God again. He has my full heart. As for my family and true friends, I love them more than ever." He might add with a chuckle, "My wife's a lot quieter now too."

LIVING WATER

"And the God of all grace, who called you to his eternal glory in Christ, after you have suffered a little while, will himself restore you and make you strong, firm and steadfast."

1 PETER 5:10

Today's Replenishment

Got leftover debris from the locust years? Carcasses
that need to be cleaned up? We all do.

It helps to start with yourself. Get some time alone
with your Bible and your journal in a place where
you can pray privately. Ask God to shine the light
on dark corners in your soul that need cleansing.
Be ruthlessly honest as you confess your sin and ask
for forgiveness. Are there any Job's comforters who
need your forgiveness too?

How about relationships that have suffered neglect?
This would be a good time to ask God's guidance
in setting things straight again. Grace begets grace.
You'll be happy you did.

Remember the eternal price paid for your
forgiveness and mine, Jesus' blood. Let's thank
Him for the rest of our lives and live for Him each
hour in the light of His gift.

Some around you are hurting badly today.
How might God want you to love
them and pray for them?

17

I'm in Way Over My Head

Toes curled at the edge of the deep end, I watched my friend Judie's orange swim cap move smoothly in the water to the opposite side of the pool. She passed the test easily. I was next. One big jump, a push off the side, and about ten good strokes lay between me and my Advanced Beginner swim badge. At thirty-five, learning to swim was like getting a doctorate.

Splash! Here goes nothing! Can't panic. Gotta breathe slowly. Take your time, Virelle. Kick, kick, kick. I heard Judie cheer. Two more breaths. Stroke. Stroke. Pull. I made it! I made it!

It was too good to be true—a lifelong dream made possible by the Red Cross swim program. Buoyed by this small success, I soon hooked a few more shallow-end friends who joined our lessons over the next two years. Together we became a flock of midlife swimmers. Two of us even became lifeguards and water safety instructors going on to teach other terrified adults for five more years.

What made the old fears leave?

Training, for sure. Cheering from good friends did wonders. But most of all, belief grew in me that I could really float, could learn, could actually adapt to deep water like others. I wasn't hopeless. Neither are you, no matter what challenge you face.

At the risk of being simplistic, isn't the Christian life like that? It starts out looking like a grand adventure. God has touched us; Christ has come into our lives and now we are free, free, free from condemnation. Eternal life shines brightly on the horizon, and the glow of God is within. But the joy of new life fades quickly when Jesus expects something too hard of us. Getting wet. Very wet.

Here's a challenge for you, dear child! Love this unbelieving mate, accept this dreaded diagnosis, leave your safe zone and follow Me! Jump in!

Eventually we jump, or someone pushes us over the edge, and we flounder badly. Maybe we even think we are drowning. Wait a minute! Where was God? Why didn't He catch me sooner? Did He really expect me to swim?

I've jumped in the deep end more than I ever wanted to. So have you. Usually, there's no choice. My deep ends looked like a prodigal son, mental illness in our family, financial tightropes, Bell's palsy, and my mother's Alzheimer's. Without God's power at work, I'd have gone under like a lead pipe. But

God kept our whole family afloat, not just me. He kept us kicking hard and learning to trust His "everlasting arms" underneath us. Now we praise God for all those deep ends.

Our oldest daughter Lauren's deep end became a marathon event with a diagnosis of lupus in her early twenties. I resisted believing it for years, until she became bedridden and needed numerous medications. Lauren never wanted that, nor did her husband, Michael. But years down the road, they've both learned to manage those waters and swim very well. It's become a praise story they'd never have known otherwise. This mama's learned a lot more, too, about trusting God with her children.

Lauren is a determined girl and a faithful follower of Christ. She persisted. She kicked hard to stay afloat and passed many hard tests of faith. For the past two years she's rebuilt her strength working out regularly at a gym. This past summer Michael and their kids and I cheered as Lauren ran in her first 5K race with her dad. Seeing the two cross the finish line arm in arm was a tearjerker.

She jogged over to us beaming. "We made it! We finished close to last, but we finished!" Yes, you did, honey. Yes, you did.

I think of the "great cloud of witnesses" that surrounds us spoken of in Hebrews 12:1 as heaven's invisible onlookers, cheering us on, praising God for our faith and obedience in the long marathons we each face.

Jesus ran His earthly race for the joy on His Father's face. He kept His eye on heaven. We can do the same thing He did. "Let us fix our eyes on Jesus, the author and perfecter of our faith, who for the joy set before him endured the cross, scorning its

shame, and sat down at the right hand of the throne of God"
(Hebrews 12:2). Jesus finished His race with joy. So can we.
When you think no one's looking, no one sees your long faith
walk, remember the cheerleaders in heaven, praying for you as
you walk in obedience to God.

The tests we face aren't for spiritual badges and trophies.
They're more like lifeguard training, equipping us to reach
those who are drowning, to do battle with a hateful enemy,
and to trust that God will hold us tight no matter what happens. That's not for sissies.

Changes in life still scare me at times, but when fear per-
sists, training takes over. It's good for each of us to take regular
inventory of our readiness to face the test.

This morning I spoke with a friend who's in a hard place
in her life. She's in the middle of a sad divorce, has gained
weight, changed jobs, is struggling financially, and is frankly
depressed. Her conversation reflects it.

After listening a long time, I asked her if she was reading a
little of God's Word and praying daily.

"Not really. I just don't have time right now." We both
knew it was an excuse.

"It helps so much," I said. "You need God's truth to take
you through this." Together we found a promise that would
help her with today's needs. I pray she'll remember to put her
relationship with God first during this hard time of testing.

Ask yourself a few questions. How are your faith muscles?
Are you regularly attending a solid, Bible-believing church?
That's where you will find the training you need to grow
strong in the faith. "Faith comes from hearing the message,

and the message is heard through the word of Christ" (Romans 10:17). If you are not in a church where God's Word is being faithfully preached week after week, consider making a change. Ask around. Pray. God will lead you.

Do you have a good coach? If not, look for a mentor who's a strong Christian, living out her faith daily. Still not sure? Ask her Maker to send her your way.

How about a cheerleader? No one likes false praise, but we all need encouragement. Cheerleaders who stick with you to the finish line are pure gold. They are usually found in a small group Bible study or prayer group. Remember to be a cheerleader for them too.

All the training in the world is useless on the sidelines. That means jump right in and get wet following Christ. He'll keep you afloat and help you pass the test with an eye on heaven. Listen! I hear cheering now!

LIVING WATER
"But one thing I do: Forgetting what is behind and straining toward what is ahead, I press on toward the goal to win the prize for which God has called me heavenward in Christ Jesus."

PHILIPPIANS 3:13–14

Today's Replenishment

■

One of God's greatest gifts to me in the process of renewal has been First Place, the Christian weight loss plan that teaches people to put Christ first in every area of life. Using their materials is like having a life coach who works with me daily. Although most First Place groups meet in local churches, I'm part of an online group led by Carole Lewis, national director of First Place. Carole is following the program right along with us. What a privilege.

Not only did First Place help me lose weight, but the daily Commitment Record helps me see in black-and-white how I'm doing. If I walk two miles, I record it. If not, that space remains stark white. When I follow the Bible reading guide, take the time to pray for and encourage others, eat wisely on the Live It! Plan, and follow the nine commitments derived from Matthew 6:33 ("But seek first his kingdom and his righteousness, and all these things will be given to you as well"), I not only lose weight, but grow strong in the Lord each day. When I don't, the result is no surprise.

If you have a trainer, a coach, and some cheerleaders in your life, you are on the road to spiritual strength and health. If not, pray about making changes that will put you in a better place to grow strong in the Lord spiritually, emotionally, and physically. You'll be so thankful you did.

18

I Feel a Laugh Coming On

I confess. I'm addicted to popcorn and funny movies. Disney films, anything rated G or PG, I can handle. Movies that speak of pain, fear, stress, violence, or smack of bad taste don't interest me at all. No matter how popular, I feel no interest in watching them. There's enough stress just living life and watching the news. Why add more?

Funny movies once satisfied an occasional need for entertainment. Now they are therapy, good medicine taken liberally during this longed-for period of renewal. I laugh without apology now, even when my laughter rings a bit too loud. It's better than a cacophonous whine.

I'm convinced laughter is a spiritual exercise. I'm told one good belly laugh daily relieves stress, boosts your immune system, and helps restore a healthy body, mind, and spirit. How can laughter not be good for you?

Few preachers mention that Jesus was possibly the most entertaining person on the planet. Thousands hung on His words for days on end, kids included. Believe me, He wasn't serious all the time. Pharisees hardly recognized true spirituality; they'd dressed it up in rules and principles far too long. We modern Christians do the same thing when we take ourselves too seriously. I've been one of them, pursed lips, intense, duty-bound. Where's the contagious joy in that?

Jesus knew how to live, laugh, tell a great story, and keep people begging for more. After all, why shouldn't He? The Author of Life invented laughter as well as truth. They are compatible. It's another good and perfect gift we often ignore.

One of the beauties of coming to the well daily, drinking deeply of God's Word, His presence, and His nature is the surprising discovery that God wants us to share His joy, not only His sorrows. He can take care of those. He wants us to have more fun, enjoy the beauty He's created all around us, and be filled with wonder and bubbled-up joy. I'm not talking about giddy or foolish fun, being careless with another's feelings or irresponsible with God's work, but rather keepers of His joy-gift within, keepers of His Light, tenders of His gospel of love and grace.

It doesn't surprise me that some of the world's greatest preachers were among the funniest. An older friend of mine used to hear A. W. Tozer preach in New York City when she was in college. "He made the audience laugh so hard," she said, "that his biggest problem was getting their attention back for the meat of his message." Crowds kept coming and disciples were made week after week.

D. L. Moody loved life and was a down-to-earth Bible teacher, magnetic, humorous, and authentic—a winning ticket. His ministry carried the gospel all over the world. The godliest pastors I've known had a well-developed, often runaway, sense of humor. Everyone listened in church. And why wouldn't they?

What is it about good, clean humor that makes us want more? It is so like God, that's what. Laughter builds a bridge to another's heart and opens the door to God's love. God is so much more than we knew.

Why does laughter matter? Its absence is one of the first indicators that something has tarnished our soul, stolen our joy. When we are badly in need of renewal, when sin has taken root in our lives, when our prayers grow dull or discouragement sets in, we seldom see it right away, but others seeking God's presence in us leave empty. That's a big loss.

Laughter came back to me like a song I'd forgotten. I hummed it all day while cleaning and packing to move, running errands, or visiting my mother in the nursing home. It sprang from the same inner joy that renewed me now, a relieved sense that God was in charge, not me, and His plans were good. Very good. I could trust them, and my song brought Him joy. Hallelujah!

Consider the fact that laughter is usually an involuntary reflex. An ill-timed chuckle reveals what we're really thinking. When the Lord visited Abraham announcing the promised miracle baby was finally on his way, Sarah eavesdropped on their conversation from inside the tent. The idea was ludicrous to her at nearly ninety. Scripture records her reaction that only God overheard. "So Sarah laughed to herself as she thought, 'After I am worn out and my master is old, will I now have this pleasure?'" (Genesis 18:12).

God was not amused. "Why did Sarah laugh and say, 'Will I really have a child, now that I am old?' Is anything too hard for the LORD?" (verses 13–14). Imagine Abraham's mortification at that.

Sarah, feeling cornered, flatly denied it with a bold lie. "I did not laugh." Before you're too hard on her, haven't we all made some totally stupid, uncalled-for comment we thought no one heard, and covered our tracks with an equally incriminating, "Just kidding. I didn't really mean it."

If you're prone to judgment, read the whole story in Genesis 18. Abraham made a blunder or two of his own.

The fact that she and Abraham later named their boy Isaac, which means "laughter," makes me wonder whether every time they used his name the memory came back. *Has anyone seen Laughter lately? I have a job for Laughter. I've looked everywhere for him. Where is Laughter when you need him?* My mind runs wild with this.

A good kind of laughter also reveals our heart. Meet the godly wife in Proverbs 31, worth a fortune to her husband, who prepared so well for the future that "she can laugh at the days to come" (verse 25). She's full of confidence in God and translates that into wise living, careful management of her household, and ministry to those in need. Do you and I have so much confidence in God that we can laugh at the future? There's no challenge we face that He cannot meet.

Sarah learned it. The Proverbs 31 woman lived by it. So can we.

Laughter born of confidence in God, of daily renewal in His Word, of joy in knowing Jesus, is the bubbled-over joy of Christ within us. I can't live without it. No one needs to.

Are you happy in the Lord today? Let your face know it. Enjoy a good laugh today.

LIVING WATER

"If you obey my commands, you will remain in my love, just as I have obeyed my Father's commands and remain in his love. I have told you this so that my joy may be in you and that your joy may be complete."

JOHN 15:10–11

Today's Replenishment

■

Scan your memory for scenes when your laughter was ill-timed or spoken at someone's expense. How did you feel when you realized your error? Have you ever been the target of someone else's laughter? In each case, what did the laughter reveal? What would have corrected that ahead of time? More compassion, tenderheartedness, grown-up faith? Does anyone's name come to mind who might welcome an apology from you? Do you need forgiveness for a past mistake? You are not alone.

How's your joy index lately? If it has been awhile since your laugh lines had some exercise, ask God and someone close to you why that might be. Deal with the root first, whether it's worry or a critical spirit, the habit of complaining, self-centeredness, or a lack of thankfulness. The joy will come when you open the windows of your soul and invite God to blow away the cobwebs and gathered dust so His Presence can shine in you once more. Laughter and freedom won't be far behind.

19

REST IS SWEET INDEED

By late March we were officially homeless. It felt odd leaving the Northeast with its gray, icy snow-banks still lining the roads.

Our old Buick wagon and a newer sedan were loaded to the gills as we drifted south, staying first with our son and his wife outside New York City for a few days, then driving down the coast to the Delaware shore where Steve's sister and her husband had graciously offered us their beach house until our closing date in Florida. There our recovery officially began. We slept late, ate fun food, walked on the beach, and explored shopping outlets. Giddy with relief, we felt layers of fatigue fall off daily.

For the first time in decades, we had no

timetable. The closing on our new home depended on plumbers and painters, carpenters and electricians finishing their work. Unlike in New York, people don't hurry in Florida. The bank inspector, whose name was Madonna, had come and gone twice with disappointing news that the work was far from done. No closing date in the crosshairs yet. After another week in Delaware, we were running out of places to go.

Sometime in April we headed to the home of our son Bob and his wife, Theresa, in North Carolina, watching outdoor temperatures rise every hundred miles. Bob and Theresa and the boys offered us refuge, though by this time we felt like two stray cats. How strange to be parents on the move, taking shelter at your kids' homes!

After hanging out at one of our timeshares, in early May we finally headed south on I-95, down the east coast, rolling across the Florida state line along with a dark storm front. As if on cue, a deafening clap of thunder opened the sky. Rain came down like the Genesis flood. I hugged the bumper of Steve's old Buick with a white-knuckle grip on the wheel of the newer car, wondering if our moving van had made it safely yet. I never heard my cell phone ring, but amidst lightning strikes, Madonna announced that one toilet and sink now worked. We could close on the condo and move in tomorrow. Hallelujah!

Twenty-four hours later we signed endless mortgage papers in a conference room while our movers stacked everything we owned in a big pile on our condo floor and covered it with plastic. Other than a storage unit still in Albany, all our earthly belongings were the size of a big snowbank.

"Of course, you know you can't actually live there yet," the mortgage broker said. "It's not fully completed—no carpet, no working tub or shower, just one toilet, and the kitchen sink."

"Oh, yes we will," Steve said with a smile. "You've never seen our wilderness camp. We can do this!"

I wasn't so sure, but move in we did. Just two brave souls camping out on twin beds destined for the guest room, one floor lamp, and some wicker chairs. Even our first apartment was nicer than this!

Honestly, it was fun. And beautiful. When the morning sun poured pink and gold into our bedroom, every window framed a palm tree. In the evening from the porch, the sunset across the street threw its orange and lavender rays in lavish abandon. We were a funny planting of the Lord amidst boxes, appliances on the porch, and workmen's ladders, but we were in our new home at last. I was instantly in love with it all. God had been more than good and we were satisfied.

Throughout the following month, we felt ourselves being rebuilt daily, just like our walls, floors, and bathrooms. The kitchen wasn't usable for a month, but the beach opened its arms to frequent picnic suppers with subs and sodas, and local restaurants along the water made us welcome. Our bodies grew a bit fatter, but so did our spirits. Each day's plans seemed simple: track down the plumber, buy towel rods, scrape the floors, pick out paint and carpet, and sort through boxes. All fun.

As our home grew around us, we grew stronger daily within its walls. Praise and thanksgiving filled us; prayers were answered in a steady stream. Living on God's new timetable, an inner rhythm was forming, as well.

Jesus showed the way long beforehand. Too bad we didn't see it. Jesus had three years to accomplish the mission His Father gave Him. Three years only. Every day the clock was ticking. Yet He remained unhurried, steadily following orders from above, taking time for those who needed Him or would listen to His teaching. I wonder, how come Jesus thought He could take time to rest? I'd have been a frenzied wreck.

He took good care of His own. "Come with me by yourselves to a quiet place and get some rest," He regularly said to His disciples. Sometimes, the mobs found them, begging Jesus to teach and heal more. And He did. (See Mark 6:31–34.) The wee hours of the morning often found Jesus seeking time alone in His Father's presence. He needed renewal just like you and me.

Apparently, regular rest mattered a lot to Jesus. No one has ever been busier or more important, including any sitting president or pope. Jesus practiced a different kind of rest, something so obvious I had missed it.

Look around you. Who is taking regular time to rest? Practically no one. I certainly wasn't. Are you?

But rest goes deeper, doesn't it? Jesus found rest in an inner posture of submission to His heavenly Father, a poised state of body, mind, and soul in balanced oneness with His purposes. That can't happen reading a devotional for five or ten minutes a day, but in withdrawing to be alone with God.

Picture a well-trained athlete or an accomplished musician, high achievers for sure. Without the rhythm of renewal and rest, their demanding life would outstrip their strength. To achieve our best for the Master, we need periods of renewal right down to our toes.

More than once Jesus has called me to stop striving with these words: "Come to me, all you who are weary and burdened, and I will give you rest. Take my yoke upon you and learn from me, for I am gentle and humble in heart, and you will find rest for your souls. For my yoke is easy and my burden is light" (Matthew 11:28–30). When I forget, eventually His love stops me and carries me to a quiet place to rest and remember again.

LIVING WATER

"Let the beloved of the LORD rest secure in him, for he shields him all day long, and the one the LORD loves rests between his shoulders."

DEUTERONOMY 33:12

Today's Replenishment

Do you have any memories from childhood of
being carried on your daddy's shoulders? That's the
picture today's verse gives me. Even though I can't
remember my earthly daddy doing that, my
heavenly Father carries me all day long on His
shoulders, just as He carries you. Think about it.
You and I are perfectly safe up there.
And what a view!

Has it been a while since you rested and were
refreshed in God's presence? Why not write out a
prayer telling Him about the closeness you long
for? Ask for a renewed sense of being carried on His
shoulders. Something wonderful happens when
God ordains real rest for us. He makes the time
and place and intends to join us Himself.
And God always brings the food.

Rest is a gift God gives His tired children.
It is not retirement from His service. Not at all.
God offers renewal for our next assignment.
Never feel guilty when He provides a rest like that.
You need it. So do I.

20

RECOVERING A HAPPY HEART

Waking up morning by morning in a sunny climate became an invitation to live again, to learn and grow and try new things. And we did. The 8:00 a.m. tennis crowd, some of the most fun and patient people on the planet, soon coaxed us to join them. As I write this my right shoulder is still sore. Not long ago we bought a baby sailboat from Pete, our favorite tennis expert, and are learning elementary navigation on the nearby Indian River Lagoon. Dolphins and manatees, turtles and tarpon, alligators and sharks all call it home.

Steve had studied stone carving over the past several years at an art institute in the Northeast, completing a marble angel that still amazes me, as well as a few pieces still

in the works. One day we drifted into the Vero Beach Art Museum and felt like we'd come home. Beauty welcomed us in each sunlit gallery, but most of all, my husband found a place to pursue sculpting again. He signed up for a class on bronze casting. I had no idea I would learn so much just watching him.

Steve's enthusiasm is contagious. When working on a new project, he takes over the whole kitchen, melting wax in hot water in the sink (a big problem until he lined it with a plastic garbage bag), carving the wax with special tools into an angel, then transporting his newborn baby to the studio in a soft-sided cooler.

One morning Steve invited me to watch the casting of his "Praising Angel," one of his first pieces in bronze. The art studio was located in an airy cement-floored building housing smoking furnaces, sand pits, several large kilns, and a fiery crucible built into the floor. It looked almost medieval. Local artists dressed in heavy leather aprons and welders' gear readied their work, like laborers in a foundry.

"Six thousand years they've been doing it like this," said Val, an expert bronze caster with a gray ponytail. Darting around the fire-breathing machines, he shouted over the noise of the bellows, "It's called the 'lost wax technique.' This kiln melts the wax inside the silicone-coated pieces. Wax goes right down into that pan of water below the kiln, like a big flat pancake." Steve's angel was set into the flaming kiln with other orange "brothers." It was closed and flames soon shot out the bottom as melting wax streamed into the water pan beneath with a hissing, breathing sound.

"We get some big fires going in this place!" Val said with a grin. "Want to look inside the crucible?" He handed me welder's headgear. I put it on and peered gingerly into the flaming twelve-inch-wide hole on the floor. Flames glowed green over the white-orange cavern where bronze ingots melted in a pulsating lake. The light's intensity hurt my eyes; the heat penetrated my clothing instantly. I backed away, wondering if this was what hell was like.

The head sculptor approached the fiery opening with long black tongs, fished something out, and dumped it on a small metal table where it throbbed orange and glowing. "What's that?" I asked Val.

"Just the dross. When the bronze is hot enough, we pull it out and throw it away. Yup, we're just about ready now. Better stand back."

The kiln opened to the glowing orange "brothers," which were carefully lifted out with long black tongs and rolled in a wire cart over to a long sandbox. Val made a trench down its length and placed each upside down in its own spot where it waited to be filled with molten bronze.

I moved carefully around the periphery photographing this ancient ritual of beauty by fire, barely breathing as two leather-clad artists lifted the glowing crucible high above the furnace with a long-handled two-man holder. Moving down the sandbox, they poured the brilliant orange liquid carefully into the shell of each waiting piece, birthing a lighted parade, Steve's small angel among them.

I felt as if someone should pray and dedicate these pieces to the Lord.

"How soon can we see them?" I asked.

"Oh, soon. Tomorrow for sure. They still need grinding and polishing, of course."

Of course. Grinding and polishing follow the crucible. Too bad for the orange brothers.

When it was time to go home, I hated leaving Steve's angel behind. I drove home lost in thought.

We'd felt the kiln and the crucible several times. We must have had a lot of dross, a lot we needed to leave behind. But this time, when God lifted us out, He set us in the Florida sand to rest and be filled anew. What a merciful God! Each new day we felt His life pouring in, recreating us into a new shape, having no idea what grinding and polishing lay ahead.

Before today, furnaces and crucibles always seemed bad places to me. I pictured Shadrach, Meshach, and Abednego, young men bound and thrown into a fiery furnace by King Nebuchadnezzar of Babylon. How evil! Yet what happened next? Old Neb peered into the flames and squinted. "Weren't there three men that we tied up and threw into the flames?"

"We certainly did," his advisers chanted (sorry, VSV again).

"Look! I see four men walking around in the fire, unbound and unharmed, and the fourth looks like a son of the gods" (Daniel 3:25).

Don't you wish you could have been there when Neb called them out and saw them whole, not one hair on their heads nor thread on their clothing even scorched? No one expected Nebuchadnezzar to become God's ally, but that's what he did, even promoting Shadrach, Meshach, and Abednego to positions of authority.

Where is God when we are thrown into the flames? He's there with us, between our flesh and the fire, sharing our sorrow, walking with us. Who but God can bring radiant beauty out of your crucible and mine? Unknown to us, He is also speaking to a pagan world that watches our suffering and wonders if God will deliver us. I've met many whose stories after the crucible have made them more beautiful, and so like God. Will He do less for you and me?

Lift me from these flames, Lord, when You are ready. Throw out the dross. I hate it anyway. Hold me still while You pour Your heart into mine and give me life again. I want the glow of Your presence within me. Thank You, Lord, for walking through these flames with me. Amen.

LIVING WATER

"But now, this is what the LORD says—he who created you, O Jacob, he who formed you, O Israel: 'Fear not, for I have redeemed you; I have summoned you by name; you are mine. When you pass through the waters, I will be with you; and when you pass through the rivers, they will not sweep over you. When you walk through the fire, you will not be burned; the flames will not set you ablaze. For I am the LORD, your God, the Holy One of Israel, your Savior; I give Egypt for your ransom, Cush and Seba in your stead. Since you are precious and honored in my sight, and because I love you, I will give men in exchange for you, and people in exchange for your life."

ISAIAH 43:1–4

Today's Replenishment

Are you in the crucible right now, feeling like God
has left you there alone? Do you wonder if He still
watches over you? Wonder no more.

If Christ lives in your heart today, you are
His forever. Nothing will change that.
Nothing. He will never leave you
alone in your troubles or abandon you.

No crucible feels good. They all hurt. But when we
think God has looked away, He hasn't. He's using
the heat to burn out the dross and cast us into His
image. What a privilege. A little more polishing
here and there, and you and I will reflect who God
really is without even knowing it. That's the best
way. Because after the crucible the really great part
comes: we are once again filled with joy over what
God has done in our lives. He's creating beauty we
never could have imagined.

By the way, others are watching
and are being changed too.

21

LORD, YOUR WORLD IS BEAUTIFUL!

It's hard to be around someone who's in love, isn't it? All she wants to talk about is the object of her love: how handsome he is, how flattering, how brilliant, how thoughtful, yada, yada, yada. After a while ordinary earthlings tire of this glowing monologue. But to be honest, most of us would love to feel that way again ourselves.

When I first came to Christ in my mid-twenties, I flushed just thinking about Jesus' love. I saw His hand in everything and found myself awestruck at the magnificence of a world illumined with God's presence. Since I was hungry to share my new love, anyone who brushed past me was fair game. In a word, I was obnoxious.

Decades later, I've "grown up." I'm more careful about witnessing willy-nilly. More measured, perhaps. Some call it "being sensitive." I wonder what God calls it? What do heaven's onlookers think? Probably, "This one needs her batteries recharged, Lord." Zinger! That's what real friends do. They talk to God on your behalf.

Friends of a blind man begged Jesus to heal him. "He needs Your help, Lord. He can't see!"

Leading him by the hand, Jesus walked the poor fellow outside the village. That alone was a test of faith. Then Jesus did something we'd never expect. He stopped, held him by the shoulders, and rubbed spit in his eyes. Then He touched him and asked, "Do you see anything yet?"

The blind man rubbed his eyes, opened them, and looked around. "I see people; they look like trees walking around." This must have been disappointing. Had Jesus' miracle failed? It called for a second touch.

So Jesus put His hands on the man's eyes again, then backed up and smiled. "Now do you see anything?"

"I see You, Lord! Oh! I see clearly now!" he cried out.

"Shh!" Jesus smiled again, cautioning him to keep the news quiet for a while, especially in the village, small town news being the same then as now. But off the man ran to tell his friends. Who wouldn't? You can read this story without my embellishments in Mark 8:22–26.

How easy it is to stumble around only half-seeing the world as God intends, missing the wonder and beauty of His presence. We grow stale. Tired. Mature. Our love for God grows tepid. We need a second touch. Ever wonder why?

Legalists leap to their feet and tell us, "You're not living by faith! That's it!"

Charismatics might say, "You need the baptism of the Holy Spirit! That's what you lack!"

Other well-meaning believers add their counsel. "How's your prayer life?" Or, "Are you neglecting the Word of God?"

What do you say to these helpful critics?

Nothing. Instead, watch what Jesus did with the blind man. He got alone with him and touched him. Twice.

God knows us best. At times, most of us are like this fellow. We see but poorly lit shadows of the grand Reality, missing the romance in knowing God. What can be done for us blind folk? One thing only. Simply seek out Jesus and ask Him for our sight back, perhaps a second touch.

Friends must have prayed for me. They knew I needed my vision cleared again. Do you have friends like that? Ask them to pray, and while you're at it, talk to God on your own. I prayed like this: *Lord Jesus, will You give me the ability to see others, to see Your world, to see my life as You do? My vision is cloudy, Lord, and I don't even trust myself to see anything right. I need Your eyes. And Lord, I want to fall in love with You again. Will You touch my heart once more?*

God loves to answer that prayer. Next to praying to receive Christ as Lord and Savior, this is probably His favorite prayer to answer. Every time.

What we are really asking for is Christ Himself, for His fullness in our life. We never stop needing more of Jesus. Does that imply we are not born again, or baptized in the Holy Spirit, or prayerfully studying the Word of God? Not unless

God reveals that to you. If He does, stop right where you are and make the corrections that are needed.

If you are God's child, you received the Holy Spirit when you invited Christ into your life. Spiritual growth, that mysterious process called sanctification, happens as we seek God's fullness in every part of our life. It's a continual yielding to the presence and power of Christ within us. If there is sin blocking the fullness you seek, God will reveal it. Ask Him to cleanse you and make you whole, to touch you again and restore your vision. God will fill all the empty space you give Him. Why not give Him everything?

The world we now live in is full of eye-opening beauty. Some mornings take my breath away. The birds, oh, the birds are magnificent! I call them all "Sweetheart," even the osprey that flies close overhead carrying a fish back to its nest, or the gray-faced stork that fishes in the small stream behind our porch. I'm in love with egrets, herons, ibises, and all their long-legged friends. Pileated woodpeckers scale the palms in pairs, their red crowns flashing from fifty yards.

My heart leaps each time a mullet jumps in our bay, or a silvery tarpon rolls, or a manatee looks up "smiling" from under the dock. Once I saw just grass and trees. Now I can see everything again! God made all this for our pleasure. He made raving beauties of every flame-red cardinal, hooted with laughter at the nuthatch's little "Woodstock" peep. He strung gossamer clouds in the sky and set them ablaze morning and night, and lifts the moon out of the ocean's rim to thrill us with His presence. Now I see His glory everywhere! Best of all, I see Him on the faces of His children. Do you see Him too?

Not quite? I know how it feels.

It's time for a fresh view of the One who loves you most. Don't miss it. Get outside. Get alone somewhere with God, dear one, and ask Him to touch you again. So much remains to be seen.

LIVING WATER

"But if we walk in the light, as he is in the light, we have fellowship with one another, and the blood of Jesus, his Son, purifies us from all sin."

■

1 JOHN 1·7

Today's Replenishment

It must grieve God when He's given us so much we
never take time to enjoy, or when we stumble
around in the dark, trying to live the Christian life
only half seeing the way. He has given us His light.
The truth is, there are attractions in the shadows,
and danger lurks close for all who follow Christ.
Satan seeks to devour those whom God has called
faithful. Walking in the Light is not just a good
idea. It's the only safe path.

Open your journal and ask God if He sees any
blind spots in you. All sorts of rubbish can interfere
with your vision: things like anger, jealousy,
anxiety, resentment, laziness, vanity, selfish
ambition, or anything else that mucks up your life.
Do you want to see clearly? Confess this
sinful junk and receive God's forgiveness.
Now write it down and date it.

Sometimes too much ministry obscures our view.
You may need to run out into the daylight and
breathe deeply again. Ask God for wisdom to lead
the way to a healthier balance. He will.

Now step out into the light where Jesus is.
Amazing, isn't it? Everything is beginning to look
better. Even God's family. And you,
by the way, look beautiful too.

22

JESUS, I SEE YOUR FACE!

While still in college, our pastor's son, Steve Letchford, was often troubled by one sticky faith question: Why didn't the disciples recognize Jesus on the Emmaus road? It didn't make sense. After all, they'd spent a lot of time with Him over the past three years. For Steve, it was a critical hurdle.

One day he had a brilliant idea to settle the issue. Would his own parents recognize him if he met them unexpectedly? If not, then the disciples could have been so preoccupied with their own grief following His crucifixion that they might not have known who Jesus was. A golden opportunity soon presented itself when Steve was due to visit his parents and his younger brother, Tom, in England over the holidays where Tom was studying and his parents were working in ministry.

Recruiting fun-loving Tom was easy. He was to take his parents on a sightseeing tour of Bath, his college town. Steve would pose as a student hitchhiker complete with spiked hair and a fake earring. Tom's girlfriend would accompany him in a similar getup.

When the time came, the plan worked like a charm. Tom and his parents piled into the car with his mom in the backseat. They drove through Bath, repeatedly passing Steve and Tom's girlfriend thumbing a ride. No one recognized Steve. So Tom said, "Hey, let's give those guys a ride." His dad gladly agreed. Steve wanted to sit next to his mom, so he jumped in the tiny car's backseat ahead of Tom's girlfriend, his poor manners clearly offending his mom. She could hardly look at him. So Steve said, "Hi, Mum!"

She continued looking the other way, thinking, *Wow, is this young man cheeky!* Still she didn't recognize him. Tom sat up front holding in his laughter and desperately trying to maintain composure while they carried on making small talk.

Meanwhile, Steve's dad looked in the rearview mirror and said, "My, doesn't he look like our Steve?"

That's when his mom finally turned to take a closer look. Suddenly, she screamed and laughed and cried all at once. "Steve, Steve, is it really you?"

"Hi, Mom," Steve answered in his normal voice. At first there were hoots of laughter; then the mood became serious as Steve explained how his last lingering doubt about the validity of the gospel was finally put to rest. Today Steve is a missionary doctor serving in Africa along with his wife, Sheri, and their four children. You could say his experiment worked.

Jesus' band of twelve disciples also had a seeing-is-believing problem. When Jesus spoke of "the Father," to them it translated, "Father God, who art hidden in heaven." Isn't that how many view God?

Then came the Last Supper as told in John 14. Shortly after He washed their feet, Jesus spoke tenderly of heaven, and His Father's house. "You know the way to the place where I am going." No one understood. How often Jesus must have longed for Home, and yet He remained here to seek and save His lost children.

Thomas, ever the realist, responded, "Lord, we don't know where you are going, so how can we know the way?" Don't blame Thomas. No one else knew either.

Jesus' answer startled them. "If you really knew me, you would know my Father as well. From now on, you do know him and have seen him" (John 14.7).

The disciples now sat in total confusion until Philip spoke up. "Lord, show us the Father and that will be enough for us." Yes, that would be enough for me too. Just show me Your face, Lord. Let me see You with my own eyes.

Think of it. Even after three years together, the disciples had no real idea who Jesus was. All that time they were looking at God and didn't know it. It must have taken time to sink in, and to reprocess the memories. *So that's what He meant!* His words came back in a steady stream of light.

We're no different. We want to see the Father, experience the Son, and feel the empowering of the Holy Spirit. The truth is, we have been doing so since we first believed. We just didn't know it.

Imagine the love on Jesus' face when He answered, "Don't you know me, Philip, even after I have been among you such a long time? Anyone who has seen me has seen the Father" (John 14:9).

Jesus must have spoken all this with tears in His eyes. It's strange not to be recognized by those you love the most. It was hard for Jesus, just as it is with us. If you have family members who don't yet know Christ, you know exactly what I mean.

God wants us to know Him. Not know of Him. He wants us to know Him well, even intimately.

Have you ever wondered if you'd recognize Jesus if He showed up unexpectedly today in your carpool, or on the soccer field? Would you know Him by His voice, or His facial expressions? It would be hard. If seeing is believing, even the blind man had an advantage over us. He knew when he opened his eyes he'd see Jesus.

We live as believers today without seeing Him. God knows that's difficult. That's why Jesus made an unexpected visit to cautious Thomas with the disciples after the resurrection, inviting him to feel His wounds personally. How humbling it was for Thomas to hear His rebuke, "Stop doubting and believe. . . . Because you have seen me, you have believed; blessed are those who have not seen and yet have believed" (John 20:27, 29). That would be us.

I still wish I could see Him. Don't you?

One thing I'm learning is to expect God to do the unexpected. He seldom works in the same way twice. God loves to

surprise us with His presence, like Steve did with his parents.
Like Jesus did on the Emmaus road.

I've seen God's face and not known it. So have you. So had
the disciples.

If we are made in the image of God, why should He not
appear in ways so familiar we'd miss Him? Whether a student
on the street, a refugee from foreign lands, a child without a
home, a soldier on leave, or a patient in the ER, God says,
"How is it you didn't know Me?"

God comes to us daily in the guise of those with needs. He
asks us to love them as He does, to care for them, to give His
love with abandon. He comes in the faces of children and old
people, the wounded and hurting, the grieving and lonely.
How did we not see Him sooner? Didn't he say, "I tell you the
truth, whatever you did for one of the least of these brothers of
mine, you did for me"? (Matthew 25:40).

Ahhh! Now I get it.

Yes, Lord! I see Your face more clearly now I'm sorry I
didn't recognize You sooner.

LIVING WATER

"For God, who said, 'Let light shine out of darkness,' made his light shine in our hearts to give us the light of the knowledge of the glory of God in the face of Christ. But we have this treasure in jars of clay to show that this all-surpassing power is from God and not from us."

2 CORINTHIANS 4:6–7

Today's Replenishment

■

Because we live in the anteroom of heaven, it's hard
to imagine others as God sees them. Do you ever
wonder what God sees when He looks at you? If
you are His child, then your sins are forgiven, paid
in full at the cross. That means God sees you with
the righteousness of Christ. Imagine that!

Take a look at Ephesians 1. In your journal, see
how many ways the blessings listed there affect the
person you are right now and how you look to
God. Does any of this surprise you?

Does it matter if you don't feel righteous, forgiven,
or beautiful within? What matters is the truth.
Women who are controlled by the truth grow into
His image just by believing and turning their faces
toward God every day.

23

Thank You for
Loving Me So

Hand the child in you a crayon and ask her to draw a picture of love. What would she draw? A bride on her wedding day? An unexpected gift? A family portrait? A picture of herself on her daddy's lap?

In my mind are far more framed portraits of love than I can count. Early on, there's one when I was ten of my mother making a second birthday cake and party after mumps ruined the first one. Another followed shortly afterward when she made a fire in the fireplace on an icy winter night when I had pneumonia and our furnace quit. A single mom's life is full of sacrifice.

There's another picture framing my dear Aunt Char's cozy kitchen where she regularly served Mother and me tea and homemade cookies after school, listening with smiles and interest to our day's events. Her Sunday school lesson on Mary and Martha when I was only six helped me believe God was real during my long doubting years.

Another dining room table photo shows a young and smiling Ginny and Keith Edwards, who led me to Christ and nudged Steve's forgotten faith back to life. Who can number the Christian friends over thirty-plus years who turned up on sick days or lonely days, bearing food or simply their welcome presence?

During one painful trial when my daughter was hospitalized with depression, four friends calling themselves the "Love Squad" invaded our home while we were out, restoring order out of chaos, arranging flowers in every room, doing the laundry and a mountain of ironing (which still shames me), changing sheets on all five beds, and providing a banquet for our dinner. I cried for days just walking from room to room looking at what they'd done. Others came to listen and pray. One brought a dozen pink roses. Their love spoke so clearly of the character of God that our whole family was broken with gratefulness. I could go on much too long showing you portrait after portrait.

Know what I learned from them?

People who know Christ well look alike. They are loving but not gushy, enormously patient, generous even when they own little, and always prayerful. You can count on it. These are the ones to run to, safe places in a world full of pain, grace-filled confessors who will listen without judgment and offer true comfort and compassion when needed, as well as wise and truthful words when requested. Did I mention they are utterly self-effacing and confidential to boot? People like that smell like heaven to me.

Why? Each has a story of indebtedness to Christ. Each carries an album of love portraits in her heart too, chronicling God's goodness to her. Her greatest joy is offering His love to others.

I think of so many with the scent of heaven on them: my closest friends and family, fellow speakers and writers who minister out of brokenness, my wonderful children who have borne with me through years of stress and discouragement. Their prayers and listening ears regularly lifted me through difficult days as a caregiver. How can I ever thank them? Our love has deepened, for sure. Doing the same for them now is a sacred trust.

But mostly there is my husband, Steve, who has taught me what love really is. His gentleness, encouragement, absolute lack of criticism when my steps dragged and my smiles were few, have shown me Christ's sacrificial love in a way I haven't words to explain. The love we share was given by God and has grown into a threefold cord. My life mission now is to bring joy to God and Steve daily any way I can.

If you are feeling tired and discouraged, wondering where God is, it might help to read Luke 24:13–32, a personal glimpse of two of Christ's disciples on the road to Emmaus three days after the crucifixion. It's the same story that gripped my friend Dr. Steve Letchford as a young man, and it shows Jesus taking time to interact with two discouraged people after His resurrection.

It had already been reported to the disciples that Jesus had risen, but nothing made much sense yet. Then this "stranger," who happened to be Jesus, walked up and joined them. Amazed at their lack of understanding, He explained everything to them again from Moses to the resurrection. Don't you wish you could have listened in? Read the whole passage, especially the wonderful surprise at the end.

Perhaps you are on an Emmaus road, tired and discouraged, feeling God has let you down. He didn't do what you expected, and now you're not sure what to believe. We've all walked that road.

Wait awhile. Walk a little farther. I pray soon you'll make the same wonderful discovery the disciples did, that God was close all the time. He loves you beyond understanding. And He is the answer, the only answer, to everything you need today and every day.

God gives priceless love gifts in the form of those who put up with us. Beyond getting us through a difficult time, their love offers us a more authentic ministry. It's impossible to pay back God, but very possible to pass on the treasures He's given. If someone has done that for you, you are rich indeed.

My framed portraits of love are always there when I need them. At times, God reminds me to look through them again and be thankful for those who have said, "Yes, Lord," when He directed them my way. He whispers to me, "Do you remember, child, how you felt when you received My love in this way? Go and do the same for the one who needs it today."

I'm on my way, Lord. Thank You. Thank You!

LIVING WATER

*"But the wisdom that comes from heaven is
first of all pure; then peace-loving,
considerate, submissive, full of mercy and
good fruit, impartial and sincere.
Peacemakers who sow in peace raise a
harvest of righteousness."*

JAMES 3:17–18

Today's Replenishment

∎

Take out your imaginary crayons, dear friend. Who is framed in the portraits of love God has given to you? Can you name them? How about beginning your album, or adding to it, today? I will too.

As you read today's verses, do any of the qualities of godly wisdom make you wince? That's a good thing. No one has arrived in this life. God is calling us closer all the time, making us more and more sensitive to His nature. Talk to God about it with your Bible open. Write out your prayer and seek Him in His Word. Maybe you hear God whispering, "Child, let Me form My nature in you more fully. Will you trust Me completely? I want you to know Me well, child, better than you ever dreamed possible."

Will you join me in this prayer? *O Father God, make me a wise woman with all the qualities You hold dear. Thank You for sending those who know You well into my life to let me see and feel Your love in action. Bless every one of them, Lord, especially those who were unaware their lives shone for You so brightly. Father, for those who need one like that, please send someone to show her Your love today. In Jesus' strong name, Amen.*

24

SPRINKLE ME WITH JOY AND WONDER

When our grandkids visit us in Florida, nothing equals their enthusiasm over our new environment. Whether hunting lizards that dart on every walkway, or fishing tarpon on Papa's dock, or watching the mullets jump in the bay, they help me capture the wonder I've missed and hold it a moment in my hand.

Children are wired to enjoy life. Jillian at six set the standard for the most tireless fisherman in the family. She made her daddy Michael proud. Thane, her almost nine-year-old brother, matched her exuberance by playing golf whenever possible. At two, Kerith could hardly sleep, she was so excited to be here every day.

This fall their cousins, ten-year-old

Logan, eight-year-old Samuel, and two-year-old Noah on their first visit were so consumed with the limitless adventures that we had to beg them to stop and eat. It made me laugh hearing their parents say, "No more lizards today, Logan and Sam. We have to go to the beach." Or how about this: "Papa has to rest now. He's exhausted from all this fun!" What a world away from our nose-to-the-grindstone life a few years ago!

As I write this, I'm gearing up for our smallest family fry. Jack, who turned one this week, arrives on Thanksgiving with his Mommy and Daddy and another one "in the oven." What fun it will be seeing life through Jack's eyes.

I think Jesus enjoyed children the most because they hadn't lost their wonder and joy at the world He had made. Kids look at life and God with wide-eyed honesty. The problem is that by the time they're eleven or twelve, heartaches and responsibilities have nearly knocked the wonder out of most children. Nothing is sadder than talking with a cynical child.

The good news is, it's not too late to get your wonder back. Any child can point the way. My grandchildren's sense of adventure jars my lethargic soul and begs me to plug it in again. It always takes energy, but it's never dull. Plugged-in life is not self-centered. It's God-centered, full of light, and wide awake.

I'm convinced God intends His children to be filled with joy, deep inner satisfaction, not only at who He is, but at what He has made. Suppose all this were a 3-D picture of heaven and we missed it? Imagine our shame when we arrive Home to His disappointed words, "Why didn't you enjoy it more? Didn't you marvel at all I made for you?"

Grown-up minds often regard a child's world as meaningless play. Quite the opposite. Children take discovery seriously. Imagination is one of their best tools. God joins them while they make a camp in the woods, see a hero or princess in the mirror, play with dolls, create paper villages and airplanes, or practice hanging upside down from tree branches. He delights in watching little boys sitting on bridges snatching carp, studying an anthill, or thatching their first fort with poison ivy. Children often feel God's presence at play, though they can't capture it with words and may never tell anyone. This child talked to Him daily as her best friend, but it was years before she knew who He really was.

Remember back to the wonder years of your childhood. What thrilled you, challenged you, called to you? Try to remember the hours you spent happily alone. My older brother Roger built elaborate villages out of paper. Steve fished alone for hours sitting under a bridge over the Conewango Creek, mesmerized by huge carp swimming by. What kept you marvelously occupied? Now picture God's presence there with you, as indeed He was. You just might not have known it.

When Jesus invited a small child onto His knee, he met no resistance. Kids were relaxed and happy there, finding Him familiar, loving, and unhurried. He often used them to illustrate great faith to calculating adults. "I tell you the truth," He said with His arm around a small child, "unless you change and become like little children, you will never enter the kingdom of heaven" (Matthew 18:3). I can hear throats being cleared all around the crowd. *What's He talking about? Doesn't He know we are teachers of the law?*

Jesus loved challenging religious types. He went on, "Therefore, whoever humbles himself like this child is the greatest in the kingdom of heaven" (Matthew 18:4). This probably didn't sit well. Neither did His next words, "And whoever welcomes a little child like this in my name welcomes me" (verse 5). Now His expression changed; His voice lowered. "But if anyone causes one of these little ones who believe in me to sin, it would be better for him to have a large millstone hung around his neck and to be drowned in the depths of the sea" (verse 6). In a world where children were to stay in the background and not interfere with important adults, these were radical words indeed.

More than nice sentiment about children, Jesus' words are best regarded as words to live by. How do we change and become like little children again?

For me it means to receive life daily as a gift from His hand. It means to rest quietly on His great lap, knowing my Father has everything that concerns me under control. He will never leave me or forsake me. I am His child forever, and He my Savior, Friend, and Father. I need nothing He will not provide. On His lap, I live close to His heart, near His ear, able to hear His softest whispers.

Long after I came to know Christ as my Savior as an adult, my memory bank cracked open one day to a painful moment in my childhood. I was about seven and my father had just left us. He suffered torment from mental illness, as yet untreated, and moved our family every year to a new home in a new location. My father's life created havoc in our home, but I still loved him. I may have been the only one who cried when he left.

I remembered sitting on the corner of my bed, perhaps kneeling there, crying over losing him. I knew he wouldn't be back, and facing the future frightened me. God allowed me another visit to that scene now as a believer. He let me "see" that He was with me that day, comforting me, caring for me and those I loved. He was also with my father, none of which I could have known at the time. I could now close the door on my childhood pain and unanswered questions, knowing with thankfulness that God was there, though I knew it not.

Like any loving parent, God finds His greatest pleasure in His children's closeness and trust. We feel that pleasure ourselves when we do what matters most to Him: loving Him back by loving others, praying for those who hang in the shadows, living each day with wonder and joy, thankfulness and praise.

Fill me with wonder and joy again, Father. Open my eyes to see Your world as You want me to. Help me not to miss Your fingerprints all over it. I rest my life in Your great lap today. Thank You for inviting me so close.

In Jesus' strong name, Amen.

LIVING WATER

"As the Father has loved me, so have I loved you. Now remain in my love. If you obey my commands, you will remain in my love, just as I have obeyed my Father's commands and remain in his love. I have told you this so that my joy may be in you and that your joy may be complete."

JOHN 15:9–11

Today's Replenishment

∎

When I was a child, I seldom played with dolls
other than to cut their hair. (I still love cutting
hair.) Instead, I played with cowboy hats and guns.
My husband carries a faded black-and-white photo
of me at age eight or nine sitting on the fence in
front of my house holding a pair of six-shooters. It
was my everyday outfit on many cowgirl
adventures in the woods behind our house. I knew
every inch of those woods, every trail, especially the
left-hand fork past the blackberries and up a long
hill. That's where my girlfriend Barbie and I often
played. It was also a small sanctuary where I talked
to God on my own.

Can you remember a place like that? Have you
good memories in your treasure chest of places
where you first felt wonder and awe at God's
creation—possibly at the ocean, or at camp, at a
friend's farm, or fishing on a lake? If so, write it
down. Recapture the sensations if you can. God
was with you as a child, even if you were treated
badly by those who should have loved you, even if
your trust was broken too many times. God was
near and He grieved. We have no idea how much
He really intervened, do we?

Perhaps you should ask God today to help you "see"
His presence in painful moments in your own life,
when you felt so alone but were not. List those times
in your journal today and write a prayer of response.

25

LORD, YOU ARE MY WELL

It seems so long ago since my friend Liz handed me her "God-told-me to give this to-you" note. Its message was simple, "As they make music they will sing, 'All my fountains are in you'" (Psalm 87:7). At the time, I thought God wanted me to praise Him more, to sing in my heart to Him throughout the day. As I did, I felt freer, happier, less fretful. But there was more to the message. Far more. It took me years to uncover the treasure inside.

Like many new believers heady with budding faith, I ate up Scripture like a starving person and, in my humble opinion, seemed to learn everything quickly. But the longer I've followed Christ, the more I realize I've barely brushed the surface of God's truth.

I'm sure God never intended His children to be dense. We got dull on our own. Jesus frequently marveled at the sheer slowness of His disciples to "get it." Thankfully, He never minds when we ask, "Could you explain that just one more time slowly?" I recited Liz's gift verse over and over for years trying to "get it" before asking God to explain it to me slowly.

He did just that.

Slo-o-o-owly.

For years God led our family up one mountain and down another. He comforted us in heartbreak, carried us through our worst nightmares, fed us in times of famine, and feasted us with unexpected gladness. He partied with us, entertained with us, laughed and cried with us, and led each child safely back to the fold when they wandered, which amazes me to this day. Amen and amen.

Jesus gives good gifts every time we ask. When I finally asked for understanding of Liz's verse, He showed me He'd been giving it all along. Aha! I'd missed it.

Want to know what I learned? Brace yourself.

Here it is: Jesus *is* the well. He's also the Living Water in it. He opened the Way at the cross, lived and taught Truth fleshed out, and offers resurrection Life to all who come to Him and drink. Jesus is the whole package, beginning to end. Alpha and Omega. The whole chorus of heaven resonates with this song: "all my fountains are in You."

Simple, perhaps, but profound for me. I wonder, why didn't I get it on my own? I think it's because Jesus teaches best through stories, including our own. He's a show-and-tell God who loves His children too much to hurry them. Instead, He leads them gently, giving them Living Water along the way. The Good Shepherd can do that. But He's the only One who can.

What does this mean for you and me? When we are dragging ourselves through personal drought, begging for relief and rest like I was, He brings the Water of Life! When we feel faint from exhaustion, He is the Bread of Life. Jesus is all we need, whenever we need it. We simply have to ask and open wide.

Are you out of strength? Ask for more. Need direction? He will take you there. Anxious over tomorrow? He's got it all under control. Ask Him for peace. Whatever we need, when we ask, He gives us the best there is—Himself! Jesus is the answer to every thirst known to man. You and I have no need He cannot handle. The trick is, when we pray, "Lead me, Lord," He will. But He will not explain what He's doing or ask your permission. That's how faith grows on the journey.

If we will ask, God will provide exactly what we need, when we need it, and not a second sooner. He gave me rest on the day I simply couldn't go on. Many have similar stories of eleventh-hour miracles that arrived the moment they were needed.

God has supplied me over the years with women of deep faith who became surrogate moms. They added a biblical dimension to the motherly love I had already received from my own mom. One of them is Ruth Camp, mother of my dear friend Judie. Ruth is now in her late eighties and a magnet for countless people like me who hunger for the wisdom and humor that flow from her. I called her recently for purely selfish reasons.

"Hello!" Her musical voice always blows me away. I thought she was her daughter. "Oh, no, Virelle. It's just me. Did you want Judie?"

"Not this time, Ruth. I just wanted a Ruth fix. How are you, dear lady?"

"I'm just an old lady in love with God."

That's what I want to be someday! An old lady in love with God. *Thank You, Lord, for putting Ruth's bright example in my life.* We chatted awhile, catching up on her family's news. "Now, tell me how you really are," she said. "I want the whole story." And I told her. I knew I would.

Ruth bears a drink of Living Water for my soul. She's the woman God spoke of in Psalm 92:12–15: "The righteous will flourish like a palm tree, they will grow like a cedar of Lebanon; planted in the house of the LORD, they will flourish in the courts of our God. They will still bear fruit in old age, they will stay fresh and green, proclaiming, 'The LORD is upright; he is my Rock, and there is no wickedness in him.'"

I want to be like that. How about you? It starts at the well, finding all our fountains in Him. He'll give you a song that's yours alone to sing for His glory. You never know who needs it desperately.

LIVING WATER

"For the Lamb at the center of the throne will be their shepherd; he will lead them to springs of living water. And God will wipe away every tear from their eyes."

REVELATION 7:17

Today's Replenishment

■

Eleventh-hour answers to prayer are not given just
for our own needs, but to be shared
with others. Write them down.
Rehearse your story as God directs.

If you've never prayed through a psalm, making it
your own, this is a perfect time. Try praying
through all of Psalm 103. Thank God for every
love gift He's given, especially those you didn't
recognize at the time.

Do you have a Ruth in your life? If so, you're rich.
Why not tell her how much she's given you? Send
her a card or note expressing your thanks. We
forget that mentors need encouragement too.

Possibly you *are* Ruth for someone else, maybe
many others. That's even better. Ask God to keep
you faithful and true, to keep your feet from
slipping. Regularly pray for those He's placed in
your sphere of influence, thanking Him ahead of
time for the song He is developing in their lives.

26

FILL ME WITH
LIVING WATER FOR OTHERS

In June 2002, I was given a timeless treasure: an expenses-paid trip to Israel for ten days as a guest of the Israeli Ministry of Tourism. But for me, the offer had a flip side: fear. Israel was again rife with daily bombings, blood flowing on the news each night.

Steve called to confirm the invitation while I was speaking at Worldview Church in Cleveland, Ohio. "Steve, what if I don't come back?" I cried over the phone. Could I risk not seeing him again, or my children and grandchildren?

"You have to trust God," he said gently. "If it were me, I'd go."

Debbie Roberts, a pastor's wife and a five-star encourager in my life, had left a CD

in my hotel room of original worship music recorded by members of the Cleveland Symphony who attend their church, "just in case you need it for prayer." I turned it on and fell to my knees by the bed, soon weeping as the presence of God spoke gently to my need. *Why are you afraid, Child, of the next thing I have for you to do?*

Would I not receive this good gift from His hand, no matter the outcome? Was I not His own in Israel as well as here?

I was. I would go . . . and with a thankful heart. It amazes me now to think I might have stayed home and spent the rest of my life regretting it. I am grateful to Steve and Debbie for their encouragement. Sadly for us, about two years later, Debbie suffered a cerebral hemorrhage and left us for heaven, still young and beautiful in her forties. I miss her still.

Six of us, mostly Christian women journalists, landed at Ben Gurion Airport in Tel Aviv, shuffling our papers through security. Once we were out in the bright sun, our guide, Miriam, greeted us with her smile and clipboard while our Danny DeVito-style driver whom no one will ever forget stuffed our luggage into a long white van. We squeezed in and were off.

The next morning, feeling anything but refreshed, we headed east along endless patchwork fields. Mountains rose to our left and Armageddon, scene of the last battlefield in the world, stretched far to our south. Miriam sat in front spilling more information than we could take in. I rode in the back with Dana, the spirited organizer of our trip.

We finally arrived at Tiberias, exiting the tightly packed van by unfolding ourselves backward one row at a time. The Sea of Galilee, wide and long and deep, encircled by moun-

tains, sparkled before us. It took my breath away. Anchored
nearby were several ancient-looking boats, modeled after those
used in Jesus' day. Other than the cars near our hotel, the sin-
gular landscape might not have changed much in two thousand years. In a strange way, Israel felt like home.

Hard to fathom, but here we stood in Galilee where Jesus
grew up, called His disciples, walked and taught, healed the
sick, ate with family and friends. It became my favorite place
in Israel. These hills and rocky paths that framed its ancient
shores now called to deep places in my soul. God's handprints
are all over Israel, and on you and me too.

Miriam's commentary flowed. "The Sea of Galilee is the
water source for all of Israel," she said. "Its levels are carefully
monitored daily. Water is, indeed, life in a desert land. No one
takes it lightly." We take fresh water for granted, but that's not
the case in much of the world, particularly countries with few
water sources, like Israel.

Imagine what it sounded like when Jesus sat by the well
and said to the woman, "If you knew the gift of God and who
it is that asks you for a drink, you would have asked him and
he would have given you living water" (John 4:10). A bizarre
statement, indeed. No one would claim such a thing unless
He were mad, or truly the Messiah.

We know the result. The outcast dares to believe Him, and
immediately runs to tell the whole village where Jesus can be
found. She becomes what each of us, having drunk Living Water, are designed to be, water bearers for others, just as Jesus
promised: "Whoever believes in me, as the Scripture has said,
streams of living water will flow from within him" (John

7:38). The best part is, we don't even have to know when it's happening. God does it. Not us.

Somewhere in our hardwiring as people made in the image of God, we must share a deep need to find the true meaning of life. Some call it a "God-shaped vacuum" longing to be filled, or simply a desire to hit the mother lode of truth. Many religions offer alternate paths that lead nowhere. You may have dabbled in a few, things that sounded feasible at the time.

I was never a good history student, but I do remember as a kid thinking Ponce de Leon's quest in the New World for the "fountain of youth" very strange indeed. Maybe he thought he'd never have to get old and die once he found it. Now I'm a grandmother living in Florida and I've discovered the search still rages on here, way beyond the sunshine and endless beaches. Plastic surgery, cosmetic dermatology, exotic health spas, weight loss cures, you name it. We've got the corner on it. America craves youth and beauty, and Florida is one state knocking itself out to provide both. (Not that any of these are bad within limits. My son just treated his wife, José, and me to a facial and massage at a nearby spa. I loved it!)

Jesus is our Source, our Galilee within. He gives us the same water-bearing ministry to others dying of thirst. Hallelujah! What a joy! Even though we experience times of exhaustion, discouragement, or depression, Jesus never leaves us for a moment. Neither will His springs ever run dry. We have only to drink deeply, soak it in, rest, and be refreshed.

LIVING WATER

"The LORD will guide you always; he will satisfy your needs in a sun-scorched land and will strengthen your frame. You will be like a well-watered garden, like a spring whose waters never fail."

ISAIAH 58:11

Today's Replenishment

In your mind's eye, picture what it must have meant in Jesus' day for the Source of Life to be walking unrecognized among people. Here was the Creator of the world, the Author and Finisher of our faith, the Word made flesh, their longed-for Messiah, the King of kings and Lord of lords, the Savior of the world. Jesus was far more than anyone dreamed of rolled into one solid, very real human being who was also God in the flesh.

You and I live on the other side of the Cross. Once we invite Jesus into our lives as Lord and Savior, we know Him for real. Consider how many ways this fills the deep longing in you for the Truth. In your journal, list as many ways as you can. The gospel of John records Jesus telling us over and over who He really is. Picture Him like that.

Now, how much have you drawn from the Well? What do you need today? Will you write out a prayer and ask Him? He delights to give living water in abundance.

PLEASE OWN
MY RENEGADE TONGUE

My third-grade teacher stopped me on the way to lunch one day and said quietly, "Virelle, you need to think before you speak."

I stood mystified a moment, but agreed to try. I didn't know anyone could do that. Could mouths and minds work separately? Mine couldn't. It would be a lifelong theme.

Fast-forward twenty-plus years. My ten-year-old daughter listened intently to my apology for an outburst of anger and answered, "Mom, if you thought before you spoke, you wouldn't have to do this so often." I was hearing my third-grade teacher all over again. Would I never learn?

I'm now in the last third of my life.

Maybe later. After praying decades for God's control over my tongue, I'm much better than I used to be, but a long way from the quiet, gentle spirit I admire so in others. I will never be shy, my laugh rings louder than most, and I tend to speak very honestly, maybe too honestly. But now, I'm certain I had it right in third grade. The mind and mouth do act together, after all. The deal is who owns them.

If God doesn't own me fully, the whole package, my tongue will never be under His control. It will seldom bear living water for others, seldom be a blessing, seldom offer praise and worship as God desires. Does that make you squirm too?

It's a universal problem for all believers: what comes out of our mouths is what's inside. "We all stumble in many ways," says James, the Lord's natural brother. "Those who are never at fault in what they say are perfect, able to keep their whole body in check" (James 3:2 TNIV). Apparently James had problems too. Much of his writing is about the power of the tongue to heal and build, or tear down and destroy.

When busyness and distractions crowd out my daily time at the well, my whole being reflects it. The sweetness of Christ's fellowship early in the day isn't fresh on my heart. It's no wonder I soon feel out of sorts and dry, and my words show it. You too?

Shake a glass of milk, and milk will spill out. If vinegar is in there, guess what will come out? If Jesus is Lord on the inside, whether we're shaken, stirred, or broken in bits, His person will come out; His love will express itself; His expression will be on our faces. It can't be otherwise.

That may sound simple, but it isn't. Inside us is a self-centered toddler constantly tapping our leg until we get to heaven. When a toddler is in control, the result is havoc. The same is true in our Christian life.

God always honors the desire of our hearts to obey. He helps us by quieting the toddler inside, cheering us on, opening the next door. Start small. Ask God to help you obey His very next prompting. Just one thing at a time. Obey and celebrate His pleasure!

Enjoy the Fatherhood of God. As a child from a single-parent home, I longed for my father when he left. When God opened His arms wide on the cross, heaping the payment for my sins on His own Son, I ran to meet him. A Daddy at last! First John 3:1–2 became one of my favorite texts.

> How great is the love the Father has lavished on us, that we should be called children of God! And that is what we are! The reason the world does not know us is that it did not know him. Dear friends, now we are children of God, and what we will be has not yet been made known. But we know that when he appears, we shall be like him, for we shall see him as he is.

God wants us to know Him as Father and enjoy Him daily, as He longs to enjoy us. In the process, we become like Him. Our words reflect Him, as do our face and our thoughts. That's what we were made for.

"Listen and understand," Jesus said to the crowd around Him. "What goes into your mouth does not defile you, but what comes out of your mouth, that is what defiles you" (Matthew 15:10–11 TNIV). Bad news indeed. Words coming out of our mouths are far more serious than donuts going in. Donuts aren't good for you and, yes, they put on pounds, but they won't kill you. Untamed words, however, can poison relationships, destroy marriages, slay fragile hearts, smear the image of God, and weaken others' faith. The power of words lasts for eternity. How have others' words affected you? Are there some that still sting since childhood? Or last night?

Wouldn't you love to become the complete opposite: a woman whose whole person reflected the tenderness of Christ? I would. What a difference that would make to those in our world. When our thoughts, our wills, our worship are permeated more and more with Christ, His words find a willing partner in our tongues, our eyes, our talents, and energies. It's as natural as a hand in a glove. Jesus fills us, His heart in ours, His thoughts finding expression in our voices, His energy creating love in motion in our world. What a miracle!

Satan can't imitate that. No one can for long. As soon as we are disturbed, the truth will spill out for all to see and hear. A person's tongue reveals what's inside the mind and announces who runs the ship. Thoughts and mouth, like two hands with one heart, both emanate from the same person.

Take a look inside. Who's running things? Listen to what's coming out of your mouth. Do you ever wonder, *Where did that come from?* If it sounds utterly unlike you, brings healing and blessing to others, leaving you and others stunned, it's probably the Lord Himself. He's having a grand time filling you with His own thoughts and words. And you will look happier than you have in decades!

LIVING WATER

*"But if anyone obeys his word, God's love
is truly made complete in him. This is how
we know we are in him: Whoever claims to
live in him must walk as Jesus did."*

1 JOHN 2:5–6

Today's Replenishment

The verses above are a snapshot of a mature
Christian: beautiful on the inside, acting toward
others as Jesus would. What's that person's legacy?
Righteousness rippling out to others, fruitfulness
from years of sowing God's love in good seasons
and dry, generations of changed lives. It's good to
ask ourselves, does that describe me? Where are my
stubborn strongholds?

Most godly people began with one decision,
honored daily. "Lord Jesus, I want Your way, not
mine, Your will, Your tenderness and love, Your
mercy and forgiveness. Fill me with Your Spirit and
show me the way. Stop me, Lord, when I start to
take over again. Keep me close to You. In Jesus'
strong name, Amen." If your desire is to know
Christ fully, within and without, you can begin
today to realize His presence in your life. Make that
prayer your own and record it in your journal. This
will be a milestone moment in your life.

28

Every Good Gift

Ten days ago, on a Saturday morning in early December, I sat in a hospital waiting room watching for the doctor to emerge from the cardio-catheterization room. An hour earlier Steve had been airlifted from our local emergency room to a heart center at Holmes Regional Medical Center in Melbourne, Florida, proving again that life can change on a dime.

Only minutes after pouring coffee that morning, Steve came into the living room rubbing his chest. "Hm-m-m. This doesn't feel right," he said, walking around the house in his navy bathrobe. I watched him head to the kitchen and take a baby aspirin.

"Let's just get it checked out and have breakfast later."

"Good idea." An unlikely response. We dressed quickly and were off. He didn't tell me the chest pains were escalating, or the pressure building in his chest. All he said, about a mile down the road, was, "You'd better drive faster." I did, never imagining a major heart attack had already begun.

All the lights were green as I sped through town, passing everyone in our way, praying silently, *O Lord, don't let me hit anyone!* In a few minutes, while I was parking the car, Steve walked into the emergency room and told the receptionist, "I'm having a heart attack." Things happened fast.

Relieved to be there, I parked the car and walked into the waiting room thinking I might have a cup of coffee. Steve would no doubt be finished soon. Thin, strong, and athletic, he's a model of health. Maybe we'd go out for breakfast later.

"May I go in now?" I asked the friendly gal at the desk.

"Not just yet. They'll call you. My husband went through this too. I know how you feel." What did she mean?

Fifteen long minutes passed before a nurse came for me. Placing her arm around my shoulder, she said softly, "Your husband is having a heart attack. We are airlifting him to another hospital. You can give him a kiss before he leaves." I was stunned. This couldn't be real, but it was.

She led me to a team of four doctors and nurses clustered around my husband, tubes and wires protruding in every direction from under his sheet. Steve looked ashen now; even his ankles were wet with perspiration. It felt surreal, like a drama in a movie. But this was our story, and I knew God was with us. I bent down to give him a kiss and whispered, "Honey, are you at peace?"

"Yes."

I held his arm gently and prayed, "Lord, take good care of Steve. Keep him close, protect his life, and show the doctors how to help him. Let him feel Your Presence. Amen." To Steve I said, "I love you, honey."

"You'd better leave now," the doctor said. "It's a half hour to the heart center. Your husband will be there in ten minutes."

Leaving was wrenching. The attendant's directions seemed simple. "Once you're in Melbourne, take a left on Hibiscus by the donut shop. You can't miss it." But crying all the way, I missed it anyway. Fortunately, before I fell apart, I made several phone calls for prayer and called our kids. An angelic handi-capped driver helped me find the hospital, and within forty minutes my waiting room vigil had begun.

Looking at my new surroundings, I thought, *This hospital could pass for a five-star hotel.* A huge Christmas tree spiraled up the three-story lobby while carols played continuously on an electric grand piano. Our first Christmas in Florida away from family, I wanted only one gift, my husband's life. A volunteer appeared with coffee and tissues and a gentle, consoling voice.

Beneath the tears, I had peace inside. We were both all prayed up, one in spirit with God and each other. Still, I prayed again. *You know we all want Steve to live, but he's Yours, Lord. You know what's best. But please, please let him live.*

Had God not given us more than we dreamed already? In the past two years alone, He'd piled huge gifts into our lap: a new life, a new home, continual beauty around us, spectacular sunrises and sunsets visible from our bedroom windows, a great church, and warmhearted new friends added to the mix.

Like jewelry from Tiffany's, God's gifts are over the top. We deserved none of it.

I often wondered what I could give back. He already had my life. Was God asking me to give more, the life of my precious husband? It wasn't mine to give. I had nothing to give but my heart: to worship God now, before He answered my prayer. "O Come Let Us Adore Him" played throughout the hospital. *I adore You, Lord. I worship You. Help me honor You in this hard hour.*

Come to think of it, this is what we are born for: to worship God, to know Him, love Him, and walk with Him day by day. It seemed so simple now. Without worship, renewal is halfhearted and temporary at best. Sooner or later, we'll be bone-dry again.

Liz's gift verse came to mind once more, "As they make music they will sing, 'All my fountains are in you'" (Psalm 87:7). Yes. It made perfect sense now. As Jesus fills me continually with Himself, His springs of Living Water must flow somewhere. Sure, they flow out to others when I don't know it, but each little drop returns back to God as a chorus of worship. Amazing! Worship in my heart births worship in others. Oh, what a gift worship is, to God but also to me. Worship renews my heart.

All God's gifts are like jewels from Tiffany's, priceless treasures showered on those who lean on Him. Salvation is a free gift. It costs us nothing but lifting empty arms to receive by faith, but cost God the life of His only Son. Prayer, the highest privilege and power of God's children, is a gift as well. And now worship, my little bit of offering thanks back to God, also pours a song of strength into my heart. Sitting there I knew, like Paul and others before me, "I can do everything through him who gives me strength" (Philippians 4:13).

Two hours later I still sat by the grand piano when a fifty-ish man in light tan scrubs emerged from the catheterization room and walked directly toward me. He offered a firm handshake and a serious expression. "Mrs. Kidder, I'm Dr. Croft. Your husband looks fit, but he has a lot of coronary artery disease. We found three blockages on the left side of his heart, and three more on the right. We opened the ones on the left with a stent and angioplasty, but the others will have to be done in a month. He's got to be on medication and make big changes in his life."

The news jolted me. This was a major heart attack. But Steve was alive! God gave him back! He gave me my husband's life, priceless to me and all our family. I knew He would take us through whatever lay ahead. This would be the best Christmas of all.

LIVING WATER
"Every good and perfect gift is from
above, coming down from the Father
of the heavenly lights, who does not
change like shifting shadows."

JAMES 1:17

Today's Replenishment

■

Do you ever look around your life, even in the midst of a mess, and see the vast number of gifts your heavenly Father has given you? In your journal, see how many you can list. It'll keep you busy for a while. Even the worst day looks better when you focus on God's unrivaled goodness.

Now look at Isaiah 58:11: "The LORD will guide you always; he will satisfy your needs in a sun-scorched land and will strengthen your frame. You will be like a well-watered garden, like a spring whose waters never fail." As you review your needs today, some may be serious, leaving you feeling heavyhearted and fearful. Perhaps you feel guilty asking God for more when you haven't lived up to what He expects.

Don't. God is honored by our trust, especially when we feel weakest. Come to Him and ask your heavenly Father to give you what is best. His love for you hasn't changed. Do you need guidance? Forgiveness? Provision? Whatever you need, be assured God loves you and will give you only what He knows is good. Worship Him and thank Him now. His springs of living water never run dry.

29

TEACH ME TO
LOVE LIKE YOU

I remember summertime church picnics as a kid at Catfish Bay on Lake Ontario. My mother even wore Bermuda shorts. Homemade casseroles, salads, and cakes framed cherished memories around painted picnic tables with the folks I loved like family.

There were always bag races for the kids while we waited our half-hour before we could swim. Someone brought sweet-smelling burlap seed bags we pulled right up to our armpits. We climbed in and lined up, each sure of winning. Hope rises high at the start of a race.

"Go!"

Huff! Puff! *Leap hard! I can do it! Only a few more feet! Ooh, no!* Bam! Falling flat on my face, I'd roll on the ground with laughter.

I'm past sixty now and still catch myself running the Christian life like a bag race, especially when it comes to loving. Pulling gumption up to my armpits, I jump in and give it my all. Until, *bam!* Down I go exhausted, hurt, or angry.

You'd think I'd learn that duplicating God's love is humanly impossible. It's the one thing we can't fake for long, and Satan can't imitate. It's deeper, wider, and higher than my small spirit can muster. Not even Mother Teresa could love like Christ on her own. Only the real Christ within us can do it. I've hit the wall many times over this, discovering again and again how opposite to mine God's love really is.

For one, His love isn't about feelings. It's not gushy, sentimental, or showy. Having little to do with money but everything to do with giving, rich and poor alike receive their supply free at the same "bank." Running out of human love is humbling, and so is asking God for His. But there's no other way.

We love like Jesus only when His poured-in love spills out. Through a kaleidoscope of ways including service, prayer, listening, speaking words of encouragement and, at times, rebuke, He directs our energies. God's love is magnetic in a surrendered heart. It draws people to Him even when we don't know it.

Need more love for others? Ask for it with a heart ready to obey. In God's eyes, love and obedience are one and the same. We can't have one without the other. That's always the rub; otherwise it would be easy. It never is easy.

Many years ago a wise woman, Jewel Hubley, listened with great patience to me complain about my difficulties with my mother. She sighed with understanding and said, "There are many solutions to a problem, Virelle, but anything next to love is only second-best. I'll pray for you. God will show you the way." Godly advice doesn't always "feel good," does it?

A few days later I stood in my kitchen in Lexington, Massachusetts, crying out, "Lord, I don't love her right now, but I'm willing to love her. You've got to give me the love I need." I'm here to tell you, He did. Within two months of that prayer, Steve's job changed unexpectedly and we moved to a new home ten miles away from my mother in Albany, New York. That was thirty-four years ago. Not only did God restore love, He refilled our bank of memories with good ones. Now that my mother is in a nursing home at ninety-three, suffering from Alzheimer's, I draw from that bank daily.

The most amazing news is how God has blessed Mother's life with a soul mate and best friend in Bill, a handsome and delightful ninety-six-year-old resident who lives on the same floor. They are genuinely happy and in love. How good is God?

The problem that dogs most of us is the expectation of returned love or at least gratitude. But God's love isn't contingent on our capacity to love Him back. Once turned loose, it is the only power on earth capable of changing another human life from the inside out. God calls it grace, totally unmerited love. Receiving grace can be revolutionary. Giving it is God-like.

Some love projects in every believer's life require input from a pastor or trained Christian counselor. If you're in that situation, make the appointment today. You'll hug yourself for seeking help. I have needed outside counsel with several challenging relationships, and still thank God for providing it.

Even if He tells you to step back and take your hands off, do it. You might be in the way.

When we ask, God's love seeps through us, uncoiling the fear, flushing out staleness, and replacing them with faith. Laying down our will is agonizing. "Yes, I will stay here as You direct, Lord." "Help me, Lord, let go of the hurt." "Be my strength. Help me keep my mouth shut." I've failed often.

Do you live with a love project? Is it a willful child or an unbelieving or difficult mate? Maybe it's a parent with Alzheimer's. Have you fallen flat yet, convinced you don't have what it takes as a Christian? Want relief?

We all fall flat. That's why we need Jesus. But He needs our hands and feet, our voice, our arms of love, our listening ears, our days and hours, our prayers, and even our money at His disposal. His power is unleashed through our small souls as He carries us to the finish line.

My heart is deeply stirred today, just thinking of the miraculous ways God's love has worked in our own family, healing our marriage in the early years, bringing a prodigal home, carrying our children through times of serious illness, mending broken hearts, giving faith and courage. Now my husband and I face a new challenge: rest and patience as he heals from a major heart attack, loving each other daily through the adjustments, sharing a 1,200-square-foot condo with few places to be alone. It's new. So far God is making it joyful. But there will be days when we'll both feel the strain.

Just yesterday we learned Steve now needs open-heart surgery in the next few weeks. My husband is easy to love, but my nursing skills are sorely limited. I'll be dependent on God daily to care for him well.

When three of our kids were here at the time of his heart attack, we sat at breakfast one morning on our porch. They talked about what a great example Steve has been to them all these years. Bob, now a super dad to three boys, expressed it well: "There's not a day that I don't think, *What would Dad do about this? What would he think or say?*" Everyone agreed.

Then I said, "I want you to know that Dad and I are okay. We feel God's love. When you go through unexpected trials, and you will, you can know the same thing. It helps to be all prayed up and at peace with one another." Suddenly an image came to mind and I added, "Kids, do you remember when you were little and Dad carried you upstairs to bed?"

"Oh, sure." They all nodded. Lauren added, "I think I was twelve the last time he gave me a piggyback ride up to bed."

"Did you ever think he might drop you?" I asked.

"Of course not!" Small chuckles followed.

"Well, that's what God is doing with Dad and me now. He's carrying us and we know He won't drop us. We're safe in His arms."

Thank You, Lord! He'd given us a picture to live with. He carries us through each day's trials, each love challenge, every heartbreak, as we ask Him to. That's all I need. How about you?

LIVING WATER

*"Be imitators of God, therefore, as dearly
loved children and live a life of love,
just as Christ loved us and gave
himself up for us as a fragrant
offering and sacrifice to God."*

EPHESIANS 5:1–2

Today's Replenishment

As long as we're alive, God will call us to new ways
of loving, and none of them are easy. Let's start
with a strategy. In your journal, list all the people
who stretch your love to the limit. They frequently
are people you live with, but not always. It could be
an irresponsible young adult, an intrusive mother-
in-law, even an abusive or critical parent or boss.

With each one, write an honest sentence or two
about what makes it so hard to love them. What
makes you feel angry and defeated? Boxes you in?
Hurts you beyond words? Be certain no one reads
this but God. (I have a friend who left instructions
for all his journals to be buried with him!)

Next, turn what you've written into a prayer asking
God for wisdom and grace to love each one. In
some cases, He will point to sinful resistance in
your own heart that requires confession. Just do it.
God can't, rather won't, answer prayer from an
unrepentant heart. (See Psalm 66:18.)
Keep the slate clean.

Now ask God to reveal His thoughts. As you study
His Word, listen to other believers, and pay close
attention to what God is doing around you;
He will lead you, even if it means
moving back to Albany!

Last, cultivate a thankful heart. Anticipate God's marvelous working in each life you've named. The best is yet to be, even if you and I don't live long enough to see it. God will answer. In the meantime, we have today. This day only. Why not pray, "Show Your amazing love to others through me, Lord. I'm all Yours, and I can't wait to see what You will do next!"

30

LACKING NOTHING

When I was in Israel a few years ago, traveling south of Jerusalem through the Judean hills, the landscape stretched wild around us, dotted here and there by small flocks of sheep, each led by a Bedouin shepherd. I counted six separate flocks at one scan. How far removed the Western mind is from the Middle East: I honestly didn't know that shepherds still "tended their flocks by night" in Israel. But they certainly do, as though nothing has changed in thousands of years.

Psalm 23, the most familiar psalm and a favorite of many, is an accurate picture of a shepherd's close relationship with his sheep. They're more than his livelihood. They're like family. Daily, as I write this book, a verse

or two from the "Shepherd Psalm" whispers in my ear. It's vividly real to me today.

Like everyone, we face an uncertain future. God reminds me, "The Lord is my Shepherd, I shall not be in want." He is looking out for His children all the time. He knows what we need and provides it right when we need it, and often when we least expect it. A friend confided that she and her husband had received a huge gift from a business associate, a freezer full of choice meat. What would they do with it all? They prayed. Nearby a single mom who barely knew them was about to receive an overflow. Our Shepherd cares for His sheep.

Following times of exhaustion and depression, my Shepherd caused me to "lie down in green pastures" and He led me "beside quiet waters." I didn't know He meant that literally! You can't get any greener grass or enjoy more quiet ponds and waterways than in Florida. This is where God has restored my soul, caused me to relearn rest, rebuilt me in His love from the inside out, commissioned me to write this book, helped me grow strong in a new season of life. How good is our Shepherd? Our well of Living Water never runs dry. He is our Way, our Truth, our Life who will never abandon His sheep.

Would He lead us on any false path? Never! He directs us only on "paths of righteousness for his name's sake." God's name and reputation are at stake in our life. What you and I do, how we pray, and especially how we follow along those paths, show God's reputation to the watching world.

Lately I've been walking "through the valley of the shadow of death" again. It's not the first time. Now I know shadows can't hurt us. When you and I walk that path with Jesus, we

really do "fear no evil." He is with us all the time. In fact, our
Shepherd blazed the path first when He died on the cross. He
died so that we could live with Him forever. What is left to
fear? His rod and staff comfort me. Why? Because any evil that
lurks along our path, He'll whack right out of the way!

One day He'll take us to a banquet table in front of everyone who said, "Where was God when you needed Him?" or,
"Why did God let this happen?" He'll say, "Sit down here,
child. I want to show you My love in a new way." He'll pour
His anointing oil all over our heads until it flows down our
shoulders and warms us through and through. Then He'll fill
our cup to overflowing with sweet wine that we'll drink in
communion with Him. That's enough for me. How about you?

Know that, even now, God will see that you and I are
rested, loved, protected, provided for, peaceful, honored,
anointed. Trusting the Shepherd, we lack nothing. He sees
that we have everything we need.

"Surely goodness and love will follow me all the days of my
life, and I will dwell in the house of the LORD forever." The
Shepherd's path is the only safe way Home. Each day, our job is
to be sure we're on it. As we study His Word and pray, He will
reveal the way one step at a time. But for now, until the day He
welcomes us Home, where our rooms are prepared already, we
have love work to do in His name. It changes from year to year.
The best news is, He gives us all we need when we ask.

Throughout the past few months with you, God has given
me a daily promise that has grown brighter and more wonderful
as I've put my full weight on it. Whenever I wonder if I have
enough to write about, or love to give, or energy for today's

demands, God reminds me that it's His to give, not mine to muster. I will lack nothing. Listen to this promise: "May the God of peace, who through the blood of the eternal covenant brought back from the dead our Lord Jesus, that great Shepherd of the sheep, equip you with everything good for doing his will, and may he work in us what is pleasing to him, through Jesus Christ, to whom be glory for ever and ever. Amen" (Hebrews 13:20–21). The power that brought Jesus, our great Shepherd, back from the dead also works in us to do God's will. Is that enough for whatever faces us today, or tomorrow, or the next day? It is for me. We can take that to the bank.

What a privilege to be His little sheep. What a joy to hear His voice, to follow closely, knowing that our Shepherd will see that we lack nothing as we do His will.

LIVING WATER

*"Consider it pure joy, my brothers,
whenever you face trials of many kinds,
because you know that the testing of your
faith develops perseverance. Perseverance
must finish its work so that
you may be mature and complete,
not lacking anything."*

JAMES 1:2–4

Today's Replenishment

■

Are you facing difficulties today that weigh you
down? What do you need to face them? Courage,
peace, a cheerful spirit, financial help, stronger
health, prayer support, a best friend? Write it all
down in your journal. List your fears, your needs,
whatever concerns you today. Put a date on it and
ask the Shepherd to supply everything you need for
doing His will. He promises that He will. How
about thanking Him ahead of time?

Often we need God to edit our prayers. Every
good writer appreciates the partnership of an
experienced editor. A bond of trust develops
between them over time. But there are moments
when the editor's red ink bites a bit and a
"discussion" ensues. Usually the editor is right,
but deferring takes grace.

Many times God has edited my prayers to fit His
better plan. It chafes, but knowing He always has
my best interests in mind makes it far easier to say,
"Okay. You choose for me, Lord. I really want
Your will in this even if it isn't mine right now.
Help me trust You." And He will.
Every time. That's good news.

31

SONGS IN THE NIGHT

Last night as I drifted off, I prayed for God's thoughts for this final chapter. Why was I surprised when, several times during the night, He woke me with the same verses, Philippians 2:12–13: "Continue to work out your salvation with fear and trembling, for it is God who works in you to will and to act according to his good purpose." I was so disappointed.

I don't mind telling you I've never liked the beginning of those verses, the part about "work out your salvation with fear and trembling." That's an uncomfortable mental picture, especially the part about fear and trembling. If Ephesians 2:8–10 is true about eternal life being a free gift, why do we need to work it out? It just didn't make sense. So I ignored that part of the verse along with others about women being quiet and covering their heads. Not my style. Until last night.

When God whispers in the night, as you may have discovered, He says important things. Waking someone up is not a time for idle conversation—something the Almighty never does anyway. After the third reminder of this verse, I lay back on my pillow and mentioned gently to Him the part I didn't like. A new thought came. Perhaps I'd misunderstood the verse! Of course, that was it! *Lord, I can be such a dunce. Help me see what it really means. I'm sorry for never asking what You meant before now.*

God reminded me that Jesus really lived in my heart, as He inhabits every child of His. Did I believe that? *Yes, of course He does. I believe that Jesus lives inside me.*

Could I picture it? Did I see Jesus alive in me daily, whether conscious of His presence or not? Well, I guess I do. I mean, of course I do.

Does it not inspire awe, a holy reverence, even trembling to be in the presence of the King of kings and Lord of lords? What would I do if I could suddenly see Him as He is? I'd fall on my face and worship!

And how would I live from that moment on? I'd do anything Jesus said. I'd want to please Him all the time, I'd want to honor Him in everything, and I'd obey Him as He gave me the strength.

Work out the joy of your salvation by doing whatever Jesus wants you to do, by living according to His will. Is that right? *Yes, Lord. That's all I want. I want to do Your will.*

Perfect. Now realize that Jesus lives in your heart daily and He directs your path according to His purpose. You have nothing to fear. He has taken care of everything. Your part is to obey and follow Him closely. That's what He wanted me to write about. *Thank You, Lord. I will.*

And here I sit with you today. What does it all mean for us, women attempting to follow Christ in a rugged, uncertain world?

The older I get, the more I realize the Christian life is unutterably simple; even a small child can "get it." The smart and savvy often cannot. Our greatest need daily is to love God with an obedient and trusting heart. Understanding that is simple. Doing it often involves a struggle, which is nothing new at all. Every saint in the Bible grew only through a struggle to work out God's will. The song follows later.

Remember Sarah's struggle with the pain of infertility, anger and doubt at God, fury over Hagar's power after the birth of Ishmael, and her laughter when God came to fulfill His promise so late in life it felt absurd? Yet did God hold back His goodness, forgiveness, or restoration in Sarah's life? Not at all. Type-A Sarah holds a place with women of faith who received the promises of God, however bumpy her ride.

What about obviously sinful women like the one Jesus met at the well? Did she not try to hide her past from God, even argue with Him over the meaning of worship? Ever notice how arguments fly from the mouths of the ignorant or unrepentant? That is, until they realize it's God they are facing. This dear woman finally stopped arguing and ran to tell her whole village the Messiah had come. Is she any less a woman of great faith than those without a spotted past? Not on your life. She's my hero.

What about you and me? When we struggle to work out the promises He's given and to do His will each day, seeking forgiveness when we fail, are we lessened in His eyes because it was hard? I don't think so.

If anything, our song is sweeter in the morning. It's sweeter when God has proven Himself strong and true, when He has restored our faith, renewed our spirit, and taken us through the high water. None of us has "arrived." Quite the contrary, are we not more aware than ever of our weakness? I certainly am. It does a lot to silence the next critical thought, doesn't it? I wonder if God doesn't sometimes favor the struggler over the "good child," like many parents do, working on her with extra care until she's obediently following the Savior, working out happily what God has worked in.

You and I have walked a shared journey to renewal this month. We've covered a lot of ground together. It wasn't easy, was it? But it was good. God is pleased at your work of faith, the trust and love you've shown, the song of praise and thanks you've sung. He has more for you and me than we ever dreamed. He has new dreams, new joys, new challenges for each of us. And one day, a new Home in heaven where we will meet face-to-face the Christ who lives within us. I'll meet you there, sweet sister. Look me up.

LIVING WATER

"My soul will be satisfied as with the richest of foods; with singing lips my mouth will praise you. On my bed I remember you; I think of you through the watches of the night."

PSALM 63:5–6

Today's Replenishment

■

Draw a line in your journal that symbolizes your life journey. It will probably be up and down, and looping around at times. Begin where you were as a child, marking off big events and turning points throughout your life until now. Can you see how God has directed your path in strange ways over the years, though you didn't know it at the time? Henry Blackaby in his Bible study *Experiencing God* calls these "spiritual markers," moments pregnant with meaning. They can be good or bad, but our life was changed by them.

You may have a handful of spiritual markers, or fifty. I have about twenty. As you think about each one, can you see how your life was altered by it? How did you feel about God at that time? How has your knowledge of Him grown over the years? Are there any events you've never "reckoned with" or come to terms with God over? Do you need to ask His forgiveness, or seek an answer for things that may still hurt or trouble you? If you need to forgive someone else, this would be a good time. Write out your prayer and date it. In order to go new places with God, you need to leave the past with Him. But there's more.

As you write out a prayer, can you thank God for
His loving presence throughout your life, creating
life where death or evil was once at work, healing
your past, causing goodness to flow from His
fountains? If not, ask God to help you do that. He
will create a song of praise where hurt once was;
He'll make a story out of every scar, a song of praise
echo from every valley. Only God can do that.
He creates strength out of struggle,
grows faith when we are weakest, creates
songs in our darkest night. Our lives are where
God's glory and honor are best displayed.

Dear Reader,

You know me pretty well by now. I hope we're still friends. What you may not realize is how much time I've already spent with you. I've prayed for you as I wrote for months, imagined your face, your needs, and wished I could talk with you. I've laughed with you when no one was around, wept with you, had many cups of coffee with you, and grown to love you very much. I hope you will write me and tell me a little about yourself. As I travel, I may meet you one day on a speaking engagement. Come up and give me a hug and say, "Virelle, remember me? I met you at the well!"

Since the completion of *Meet Me at the Well,* my husband, Steve, has had triple bypass surgery and is a champion at cardiac rehab. I became his nurse at home, but it's definitely not my strength. I'm a better soup maker and entertainer. By God's grace, we made it through those long months of recovery in time to welcome our newest grandson, Stephen Zeilstra Kidder, into the family on May 22, 2007, in New York. He joins an older brother, Jack, and a gaggle of cousins waiting to play with him. God has been so good to us.

This is our first whole summer in Florida. Yes, it's hot, but beautiful. While Steve completes his recovery, I've begun work on another new book for Moody Publishers. It's wonderful to sit here with you again, sharing the stories God has given me that make up life. In the end, they're all about Him, aren't they?

Celebrate the journey with me. You can talk with me along the way at www.virellekidder.com. I look forward to your company.

Blessings and love,

Virelle

Virelle Kidder

ABOUT THE AUTHOR

For more than twenty-five years Virelle Kidder has been doing what she loves best, speaking to audiences around the country and abroad about the love of Christ. Virelle is a "people person" who relates instantly and warmly to audiences of all sizes. She is funny, transparent, highly relatable, and solidly biblical.

Meet Me at the Well is Virelle's fifth book. A full-time writer and conference speaker, Virelle also hosted a daily radio talk show in New York's capital district. Now she's a Florida resident, still focused on encouraging women on their spiritual journey.

Virelle is widely published in national magazines such as *Moody Magazine, Focus on*

the Family's Pastor's Family, Decision, HomeLife, Tapestry, and others. Her articles have been reprinted in Australia, Germany, Poland, Portugal, Uganda, and the Caribbean islands. As a mentor for the Jerry B. Jenkins Christian Writer's Guild, she loves helping new writers learn their craft.

Virelle and her husband, Steve, have four grown children and eight grandchildren, and reside in Sebastian, Florida. They are often seen struggling wildly to dock a very small sailboat, petting manatees, or casting a line in the water.

You can write Virelle via her website at www.virellekidder. com.

For additional resources,
visit www.VirelleKidder.com

ISBN-10: 0-8024-6611-3
ISBN-13: 978-0-8024-6644-0

ISBN-10: 0-8024-6643-5
ISBN-13: 978-0-8024-6643-3

Most Christians agree that it is important to have daily time with God, but many do not know how to do so. In this companion devotional, she provides a valuable resource to spur readers on in her 30-day challenge to spend time with God. She has mined rich truth from thirty of her favorite Psalms and provided questions and suggestions to help readers develop a lifestyle of praise and worship.

Daily time with the Lord is essential for an authentic, abiding relationship with Him. But so often the details of our busy lives swallow this precious time. This compelling work by Nancy Leigh DeMoss teaches women how to have a rich, intimate daily devotional life. Readers will be challenged to transform their quiet times from daily drudgery to immeasurable delight.

by Nancy Leigh DeMoss
Find it now at your favorite local or online bookstore.
www.MoodyPublishers.com

ISBN 10: 0-8024-5278-7
ISBN-13: 978-0-8024-5278-8

Books abound for those whose marriages are crumbling or have ended. But what about those marriages committed "'til death do us part" and yet are going through a period of time when one spouse is carrying the burden? What happens to a woman when marriage gets heavy and she gets weary? Often, when a woman ends up carrying the weight of the marriage (due to her husband's health, choices, workload, etc.), her tendency is to "get out or check out." She may consider her husband's distraction an opportunity to do her own thing. But is there a better way to walk through this season? Even thrive? Susie Larson stands in as an encouraging friend, walking with you, helping you to discern how anxiety and anger will slow you down; and how loneliness and disappointment can actually refine and bless you. You will be challenged and inspired as you wrap your arms around this time and remember that God has His arms around you.

by Susie Larson
Find it now at your favorite local or online bookstore.
www.MoodyPublishers.com

Check back often to find books on . . .
Caring for aging parents
Parenting
Spiritual growth
Women's issues
and the encouragement you need
as a woman of the Word!

www.MoodyPublishers.com